Selected Essays on the Success of Mergers and Acquisitions

T0316965

European University Studies

Europäische Hochschulschriften
Publications Universitaires Européennes

Series V
Economics and Management

Reihe V   Série V
Volks- und Betriebswirtschaft
Sciences économiques, gestion d'entreprise

Vol./Bd. 3316

PETER LANG
Frankfurt am Main · Berlin · Bern · Bruxelles · New York · Oxford · Wien

Maximilian Keisers

Selected Essays
on the Success of Mergers
and Acquisitions

Evidence from the Banking
and REIT Industries

PETER LANG
Internationaler Verlag der Wissenschaften

Bibliographic Information published by the Deutsche Nationalbibliothek
The Deutsche Nationalbibliothek lists this publication in the Deutsche Nationalbibliografie; detailed bibliographic data is available in the internet at http://dnb.d-nb.de.

Zugl.: European Business School, Diss., 2007

D 1540
ISSN 0531-7339
ISBN 978-3-631-57320-4

© Peter Lang GmbH
Internationaler Verlag der Wissenschaften
Frankfurt am Main 2009
All rights reserved.

www.peterlang.de

Acknowledgements

Although this thesis bears my name, it goes without saying that its completion was made possible through the support of many people.

First, I would like to thank my supervisor and dear former boss, Prof. Dr. Dirk Schiereck, for encouraging me to undertake a doctoral research project and providing me with the opportunity to do so at his chair. He provided invaluable guidance and support during my time as a research assistant on his team and allowed me to learn from his example as both a researcher and a lecturer. I would also like to thank Prof. Dr. Susanne Strahringer, my second supervisor, for offering insightful discussions and encouraging me through difficult times.

During my two-year tenor at the Endowed Chair of Banking and Finance, I had the pleasure of working with a great team of colleagues who challenged my ideas, provided support and became life-long friends. I truly cherish that time and remain forever grateful to my peers and the entire team of the three finance chairs on floors one and two in the 'Burg' - namely the Endowed Chair of Banking and Finance, the Endowed Chair of Asset Management and the HCI Endowed Chair of Financial Services.

My special thanks go to the 'Liebig crew' - for helping me in the final correction cycle, providing moral support and simply being great friends. You will always be considered family.

I would also like to take this opportunity to express my sincerest gratitude to Dr. Walter Wagner and his team at the BWKKH Hamburg who ensured that I live to see this day.

Finally, I would like to thank my parents and my sister. Without their love and ongoing support this thesis and many other things in my life would have not been possible. Without my family I would not be who I am today.

Maximilian Keisers

Table of Contents

List of Figures _____ 11

List of Tables _____ 13

List of Abbreviations _____ 15

List of Symbols _____ 17

I Main Introduction _____ 19
   I.1 Objectives and Motivation _____ 19
   I.2 Course of the Investigation _____ 23

II Mergers of German Public Savings Banks – Case Study Evidence
against Bad Reputation _____ 27
   II.1 Introduction _____ 27
      II.1.1 Objective and Motivation _____ 27
      II.1.2 Course of the Investigation _____ 29
   II.2 Public Savings Banks – Structure and Attributes _____ 30
      II.2.1 Organizational Structure _____ 30
      II.2.2 Attributes of Public Savings Banks _____ 31
         II.2.2.1 Municipal Obligation _____ 31
         II.2.2.2 Business Policy and Public Mandate ____ 31
         II.2.2.3 Public Liability _____ 32
   II.3 Particularities of Mergers of Public Savings Banks _____ 33
      II.3.1 Possible Merger Types _____ 33
      II.3.2 Legal Restrictions _____ 34
      II.3.3 Merger Motives _____ 35
      II.3.4 Possible Drawbacks and Risks _____ 37
   II.4 Analysis of Merger Success _____ 38
      II.4.1 Prior Research _____ 38
      II.4.2 Methodology _____ 39
         II.4.2.1 Study Design _____ 39
         II.4.2.2 Merger Selection _____ 39
         II.4.2.3 Performance Indicators _____ 41

II.4.3   Stand-Alone Case Study Analysis _____   41
    II.4.3.1 Case Study One – Large absorbs Small _____   42
    II.4.3.2 Case Study Two – Distress Merger _____   44
    II.4.3.3 Case Study Three – "Normal" Merger _____   46
    II.4.3.4 Case Study Four – Multiple PSB Merger _____   48
II.4.4   Comparative Analysis _____   50
II.5 Conclusion _____   54

Appendix _____   56

III Shareholder Wealth Effects at Rival Banks: Empirical Evidence on
European Cross-Border M&A _____   57
III.1 Introduction _____   57
    III.1.1 Objective and Motivation _____   57
    III.1.2 Course of the Investigation _____   60
III.2 The European Banking Market _____   60
    III.2.1 Heterogeneity, Harmonization, and Deregulation _____   60
    III.2.2 Consolidation and Cross-Border M&A _____   63
III.3 Literature Review and Hypotheses Generation _____   66
    III.3.1 M&A in the Banking Industry _____   67
    III.3.2 Effects of M&A Announcements on Rivals _____   73
    III.3.3 Hypotheses Generation _____   77
III.4 Event Study Analysis _____   80
    III.4.1 Applied Methodology _____   80
        III.4.1.1 Market Model and Abnormal Returns _____   80
        III.4.1.2 Event Window Selection _____   83
    III.4.2 Sample and Data Selection _____   83
    III.4.3 Descriptive Statistics _____   85
    III.4.4 Event Study Results _____   88
        III.4.4.1 Bidders and Targets _____   88
        III.4.4.2 Rival Effects of Total Rival Portfolio _____   90
        III.4.4.3 Rival Effects according to Regional Proximity to
           Target _____   91
        III.4.4.4 Rival Effects according to Location of Bidder ___   93
    III.4.5 Discussion _____   94
III.5 Conclusion _____   97

IV Shareholder Wealth Effects of REIT M&A: An International Analysis   101
IV.1 Introduction _____   101
    IV.1.1 Objective and Motivation _____   101

IV.1.2 Course of the Investigation _____ 103
IV.2 Background Knowledge on REITs _____ 104
  IV.2.1 Definition _____ 104
  IV.2.2 Historical Development in the US _____ 105
  IV.2.3 Internationalization of REITs _____ 107
  IV.2.4 Particularities of REITs _____ 109
IV.3 Literature Review and Hypotheses Generation _____ 111
  IV.3.1 Literature Review _____ 111
  IV.3.2 Hypotheses Generation _____ 114
IV.4 Event Study Analysis _____ 117
  IV.4.1 Applied Methodology _____ 117
    IV.4.1.1 Market Model and Abnormal Returns _____ 117
    IV.4.1.2 Event Window Selection _____ 119
  IV.4.2 Sample and Data Selection _____ 119
  IV.4.3 Descriptive Statistics _____ 120
  IV.4.4 Event Study Results _____ 122
    IV.4.4.1 Bidders and Targets _____ 122
    IV.4.4.2 Announcement Effects according to Target Status 124
    IV.4.4.3 Announcement Effects according to Country _____ 125
    IV.4.4.4 Announcement Effects over Time _____ 126
  IV.4.5 Discussion _____ 128
IV.5 Conclusion _____ 130

V Main Conclusion _____ 133
  V.1 Key Findings and Conclusions _____ 133
  V.2 Outlook _____ 136

References _____ 139

List of Figures

Figure II.1: Net Profit Margin Development Pre- to Post Merger (Case 1) _ 43
Figure II.2: Net Profit Margin Development Pre- to Post Merger (Case 2) _ 46
Figure II.3: Net Profit Margin Development Pre- to Post Merger (Case 3) _ 48
Figure II.4: Net Profit Margin Development Pre- to Post Merger (Case 4) _ 49
Figure II.5: Development of Industry-Related Return on Equity (ROE) ___ 51
Figure II.6: Development of Industry-Related Risk Margin 52
Figure II.7: Development of Industry-Related Demand Margin 52
Figure II.8: Development of Industry-Related Personnel Cost Margin 53
Figure II.9: Development of Industry-Related Cost Income Ratio (CIR)___ 54
Figure III.1: Estimation Period and Event Window Selection 83
Figure III.2: Number of Transactions and Volume over Time 87
Figure III.3: CAAR Development over the entire Event Window 89
Figure IV.1: Number of REITs in the US (composite) and Market Cap ___ 107
Figure IV.2: Estimation Period and Event Window Selection 119
Figure IV.3: REIT Transactions included in Data Sample over Time 122
Figure IV.4: CAAR Development over the entire Event Window 123

List of Tables

Table II.1: Overview of Selected Mergers _____ 40
Table III.1: Prior Event Study Research on European Banking M&A ____ 72
Table III.2: Overview of Hypotheses _____ 80
Table III.3: Geographic Distribution of Total Rival Portfolio _____ 85
Table III.4: Geographic Distribution of Bidders and Targets _____ 86
Table III.5: CAARs of Bidders and Targets _____ 90
Table III.6: CAARs of Total Rival Portfolio _____ 91
Table III.7: CAARs of Domestic vs. Non-domestic Rivals _____ 92
Table III.8: CAARs of Regional vs. Non-regional Rivals _____ 93
Table III.9: Rival CAARs according to Bidder Region _____ 94
Table III.10: Overview of Hypotheses Confirmation _____ 97
Table IV.1: Year of Introduction of International REIT Regimes _____ 108
Table IV.2: Prior Research on Wealth Effects in REIT M&A _____ 113
Table IV.3: Overview of Hypotheses _____ 116
Table IV.4: Sample and Sub-sample Overview _____ 121
Table IV.5: CAARs of all Bidders and Targets _____ 124
Table IV.6: Bidder CAARs in Acquisitions of Private vs. Public Targets _ 124
Table IV.7: CAARS of US Bidders vs. Non-US Bidders _____ 125
Table IV.8: CAARs of US Targets vs. Non-US Targets _____ 126
Table IV.9: CAARs of Bidders in the First vs. Second Period _____ 127
Table IV.10: CAARs of Targets in the First vs. Second Period _____ 127
Table IV.11: Overview of Hypotheses Confirmation _____ 130

List of Abbreviations

AR	Abnormal Return
BVI	Bundesverband für Investment und Asset Management
CAAR	Cumulated Average Abnormal Return
CAR	Cumulated Abnormal Return
CAGR	Cumulated Annual Growth Rate
CIR	Cost Income Ratio
DIW	Deutsches Institut für Wirtschaftsforschung
DSGV	Deutscher Sparkassen- und Giroverband
ECB	European Central Bank
EMU	European Monetary Union
ER	Expected Return
EU	European Union
GPSB	German Public Savings Banking (Deutscher Sparkassensektor)
HVB	Hypovereinsbank
IT	Information Technology
M&A	Mergers and Acquisitions
NAREIT	National Association of Real Estate Investment Trusts
OLS	Ordinary Least Squares (Regression)
PSB	Public Savings Bank (Sparkasse)
REIT	Real Estate Investment Trust
ROE	Return on Equity
SBD	Second Banking Directive
SMP	Single Market Program
TRA	Tax Reform Act
UK	United Kingdom
US	United States (of America)
w/a	Without Author
w/p	Without Page
w/y	Without Year
ZEW	Zentrum für Europäische Wirtschaftsforschung

List of Symbols

AR_{jt}	Abnormal return of stock j on day t
AR_{mt}	Market return on day t
α	Regression intercept Alpha
β	Regression coefficient Beta
$CAAR_{j[t1;t2]}$	Cumulated average abnormal return of stock j (day t1 to day t2)
$CAR_{j[t1;t2]}$	Cumulated abnormal return of stock j (day t1 to day t2)
ε	Error term of the regression
j	Stock j
n	Number of observations/number of stocks in sample
R_{jt}	Return of stock j on day t
R_{mt}	Market return on day t
t	time in days

I Main Introduction

I.1 Objectives and Motivation

The international banking industry has been subject to an unprecedented level of consolidation over the past two decades and continues to change rapidly through mergers and acquisitions (M&A).[1] A few years after the consolidation trend started in the United States (US), similar developments could also be witnessed in the European Union (EU). Driven especially by harmonization efforts under the Single Market Program (SMP), such as the Second Banking Directive (SBD) of 1989 and more recently, the introduction of the European Monetary Union (EMU), consolidation activities have been reshaping the European banking industry.[2] Within this restructuring phase the number of banks decreased significantly. In the period from 1997 to 2003 the total number of European banks was reduced by 2,200 to a little less than 7,500[3], most of which is attributable to M&A. During the same period, total assets of the average bank in the EU almost doubled to a value of €3.5 billion.

The consolidation trend in the banking industry is expected to continue in the coming years as key drivers behind it push to remain in existence. First, the rapid technological progress in information technology still provides synergy potential.[4] Second, an increasingly sophisticated shareholder base as well as globalization in general push corporate strategies towards growing externally through M&A. Third, there is an implicit bank overhang in Europe and in relation to population figures, there are still almost twice as many banks in the EU as compared to the US.[5] And finally, the European banking sector continues to be the most fragmented industry on a pan-European level.[6] This provides a large potential for future European cross-border consolidation. To sum up, there are many drivers pushing banks to pursue a strategy of external growth through M&A.

---

1 Cf. e.g. Piloff (1996), p. 294, Beitel/Schiereck (2006), p. 7, and Cybo-Ottone/Murgia (2000), p. 832.
2 Cf. Altunbas/Ibanez (2004), p. 7.
3 Cf. European Central Bank (2004), p. 8.
4 For this and the next argument cf. e.g. Bank for International Settlements (2001), Belaisch et al. (2001), Berger/Demsetz/Strahan (1999), and Smith/Walter (1998).
5 Cf. Altunbas/Ibanez (2004), p. 7.
6 Cf. Serra et al. (2005), p. 1.

Concurrently, there is a lot of consolidation potential left in Europe due to the highly fragmented banking landscape.

Until present, the largest portion of consolidation in the European banking industry has occurred within national borders.[7] As a result, most domestic banking markets are already quite concentrated[8] and thus have limited remaining potential for further consolidation. Banks will therefore have to increasingly consider cross-border acquisitions if their strategy is to grow externally.[9] This development is supported by the perception that this type of transaction is becoming increasingly beneficial.[10] The consolidation trend in the European banking industry can thus be expected to shift from domestic consolidation towards cross-border M&A. Further domestic consolidation can only be assumed to occur in just a few European banking markets, such as Germany or Italy, which still exhibit comparably low concentration levels and have according domestic consolidation potential left.[11] In this respect, particularly the German public sector is expected to exhibit heavy merger activity in the coming years, which is additionally fostered by the recent repeal of state guarantees.

Similar to the banking sector, the related Real Estate Investment Trust (REIT) industry has been subject to profound consolidation. Most REIT M&A activity has historically occurred in the US, where REITs were introduced in 1960. Since then the US REIT market has grown considerably in size, reaching a total market capitalization of more than $300 billion in 2005.[12] A REIT is thereby understood as a publicly listable vehicle, of which the majority of earnings stem from real estate and, moreover, must be distributed (almost) fully to the shareholders each year in order to receive tax exemption status.[13] The REIT idea has gained increasing popularity and REIT regimes are being introduced in a growing number of nations.[14] Most recently, the UK has introduced its own REIT regime in January 2007 and Germany is currently considering doing the same.[15]

The high level of M&A activity in the banking and REIT industries and the involved transaction values raise questions regarding the success and the consequences of these transactions. Which value implications do these M&A activities

---

7 Cf. Cabral/Dierick/Vesala (2002), p. 40.
8 Cf. European Central Bank (2000), p. 18, for concentration indicators of individual European countries.
9 Cf. European Central Bank (2004), p. 9.
10 Cf. Serra (2005), p. 6.
11 Cf. Serra (2005), p. 5.
12 Cf. NAREIT (2006).
13 Cf. Campbell/Sirmans (2002), p. 389–390, Maris/Elayan (1990), p. 22, and Li/Elayan/Meyer (2001), p. 116.
14 Cf. table IV.1 for an overview of international REIT regimes.
15 Cf. ZEW/ebs (2005), p. 1–2, and Drost (2007), p. 21, 24.

have for the shareholders of acquirers? What are the wealth effects for target shareholders? Do these transactions also create value for the combined entity as they should? And finally, what implications do M&A transactions possibly have for rival companies and thereby for the industry as a whole?

A large amount of research has answered similar questions on the success of banking M&A in the US market.[16] In contrast, evidence on the European market is rather limited and there are still numerous research gaps left to fill with empirical evidence. First, research on domestic consolidation in the German public sector, which is expected to further intensify due to the repeal of state guarantees, is limited and outdated. Second, effects of European cross-border M&A on bidder and targets are also still rather unclear. There is virtually no evidence on the effects of these transactions for rival bank shareholders. And third, almost no previous research has analyzed M&A activity in the related REIT industry. Although REIT markets are spreading around the world and have grown to considerable size, no international evidence exists on the wealth effects of REIT M&A.

The three research gaps mentioned above have been identified for conducting empirical analysis, as they are found to be of particular interest in terms of both current relevance of the problem and a lack of adequate prior research. The present thesis thus follows the cumulative dissertation approach: Three selected essays were chosen, each covering a different area of M&A research. As common in a cumulative thesis, the essays are written in a publication oriented manner, i.e. each of the three essays has been written for publication purposes and has been or will be published in part (or total) in an academic journal. The essays constitute the main part of this doctoral thesis and contribute to prior research on the success of M&A in the banking and REIT industries.

Two essays cover the effects of M&A in the banking industry and the other analyzes M&A in the related REIT industry. The first essay is an indicative case study analysis of the success of four mergers in the German public banking sector. The second essay analyzes the wealth effects of European cross-border M&A in the banking industry for bidder and target shareholders and, moreover, is the first study that assesses effects of cross-border M&A on a large sample of European rivals. Finally, the third essay is the first large international analysis on the success of M&A in the REIT industry.

The following explains the motivation for each analysis in more detail and illustrates the research gaps, which the three selected essays fill with evidence.

---

16 Cf. Piloff/Santomero (1998) for an overview of prior research on the US market and Beitel/Schiereck (2003) for an overview of prior research on the European and the US market.

Essay 1:

There is a broad consensus that the strong consolidation trend in the German banking industry is going to continue, as there is still considerable consolidation potential left. M&A activity can be expected to increase, particularly in the public sector, as the European Union has ruled on the discontinuation of state guarantees (which came into effect in July 2005). Competitive pressures in the sector are supposed to have increased since then, particularly as costs for the security fund are expected to increase. Many banks seem to have difficulties in achieving envisaged performance levels on their own. As a result, an increasing number of institutions are considering merging with other public savings banks (PSBs) in order to improve profitability. A considerable rise in M&A activity can thus be expected for the German public banking sector.

The pictured consolidation trend is, however, confronted with a negative assessment of previous public savings bank (PSB) mergers amongst both researchers and practitioners. Only two studies exist that analyze mergers in the German public banking sector, both of which relied on relatively outdated data.

This thesis adds recent evidence on the success of mergers amongst PSBs by conducting an in-depth analysis of four exemplary case studies in the first essay. Similar to both prior studies, the analysis is carried out as a performance study and therefore relies on annual account data of the involved entities. Results are additionally shown in relation to industry averages to better isolate merger induced effects.

Essay 2:

The European banking industry has been reshaped by an unprecedented level of consolidation since the early 1990s. The majority of observed M&A activity thereby occurred within national borders as cross-border M&A, among other things, were perceived as more difficult and costly. Moreover, regulators and governments tried to fend off foreign bidders in order to protect domestic banking markets and to create national banking champions.

This raises the question of whether cross-border M&A are really threatening the domestic market of the target. Do cross-border M&A have an effect on the domestic banking industry? Do these transactions have an effect on European rivals as well? Finally, which implications do cross-border M&A have for both bidder and target shareholders? As mentioned before, research is still limited on M&A in the European banking industry. In addition, virtually all studies focus only on the effects on bidders and targets; there is simply no study that analyzes rival effects of cross-border M&A in the European banking industry. As a consequence, the question still remains whether cross-border M&A yield negative or positive effects on the domestic (and European) banking industry as a whole.

This thesis aims to fill this research gap in the second essay by assessing the effects of a sample of 51 cross-border banking M&A transactions in the European Union from 1990 to 2005 on bidders, targets, and a large set of European rivals. Similar to other studies, the analysis is carried out as an event study and therefore relies on daily share price data. The market model is used to calculate expected returns.

Essay 3:

The Real Estate Investment Trust (REIT) industry has experienced significant consolidation since the early 1990s and continues to change rapidly through M&A. But are these transactions creating value for the respective shareholders as they should? Interestingly enough, despite ongoing consolidation activity and despite the sheer size as well as the importance of the industry, hardly any empirical research has analyzed the value implications of REIT M&A. This is particularly true in contrast with the large amount of research covering the related banking industry. The few existing studies on REIT M&A additionally suffer from sample sizes being rather small as well as their omission of transactions in recent years. Finally, there is a lack of international evidence on REIT M&A outside the US market. As a consequence, the question still remains whether REIT M&A create value for the target as well as for the bidding firms' shareholders.

This thesis aims to fill this research gap in the third essay by assessing the value implications of a large sample of 107 international M&A transactions amongst REITs between the years 1990 and 2005. As in the earlier essay, the analysis is carried out as an event study and the market model is used to calculate expected returns.

I.2 Course of the Investigation

The course of the investigation within this thesis is organized as follows: There are five main chapters indicated by Roman numerals. The first and the fifth main chapters constitute the surrounding bracket for the three essays, which in turn resemble the main part of this thesis. Starting with the second ordering level, chapters are then indicated by Arabic numerals in order to provide a more convenient appearance for the reader.

Chapter II presents the first essay, which analyzes the success of mergers between German PSBs. Its title is: "Mergers of German Public Savings Banks – Case Study Evidence against Bad Reputation". After the introduction, chapter II.2 provides some necessary background information on the structure and attributes of German PSBs. To consider further particularities of this sector, chapter II.3 explains special features of mergers amongst PSBs. Chapter II.4 presents the main analysis in which the four case studies are analyzed in depth on a standalone basis before the assessment is carried out in relation to industry averages. The latter allows the analysis to also account for overall market developments and thereby isolate merger induced effects. Chapter II.5 wraps up the findings and concludes the essay.

Chapter III presents the second essay, which analyzes the success and the industry effects of all European cross-border banking M&A from 1990 to 2005. Its title is: "Shareholder Wealth Effects at Rival Banks: Empirical Evidence on European Cross-Border M&A". After the introduction, chapter III.2 provides some necessary background information on the historic development of the European banking industry and on recent consolidation activity. Chapter III.3 presents the two applicable strands of prior research. Prior research on banking M&A with a special focus on event studies covering the European market is first summarized. Next, prior research on rival effects is presented by focusing on the three main hypotheses that have been discussed in the literature as the source for wealth effects at competing firms. These two strands of research are then combined to develop the hypotheses. Chapter III.4 presents the event study analysis. Methodology and data selection is first laid out, followed by descriptive statistics and event study results for bidders, targets, and rivals. Chapter III.5 wraps up the findings and concludes the essay.

Chapter IV presents the third essay, which analyzes the success of international REIT M&A from 1990 to 2005. Its title is: "Shareholder Wealth Effects of REIT M&A: An International Analysis". After the introduction, chapter IV.2 provides some necessary background information on REITs. The background section includes a definition and presents particularities of the REIT structure. In addition, the historical development and internationalization of the REIT concept is outlined. Chapter IV.3 then provides an overview of prior research on the success of REIT M&A, which (in a second step) leads to the development of hypotheses. Chapter IV.4 presents the event study analysis. Methodology and data selection is first laid out, followed by descriptive statistics and event study results for bidders and targets. Chapter IV.5 wraps up the findings and concludes the essay.

The main conclusion is found in Chapter V, which quickly wraps up the main findings of all three essays again and provides final remarks as well as suggestions for further research.

II Mergers of German Public Savings Banks – Case Study Evidence against Bad Reputation

Abstract

There is broad consensus that the consolidation trend in the German banking industry is going to continue. Consolidation activity can be assumed to increase, particularly in the public sector, as the European Union has ruled on the discontinuation of state guarantees (which came into effect in July 2005). Some even expect restructuring in the public sector to be so severe that the number of public savings banks will drop to as low as 100 by 2010.

The perceived consolidation pressure in the public banking sector is, however, confronted with a negative assessment of prior public savings bank mergers. Both previous evidence and public opinion do not provide a positive view on this type of transaction. The analysis of four exemplary case studies yields a different impression and shows that mergers amongst public savings banks can indeed be successful. Three out of four analyzed transactions result in an improved ROE in relation to the public sector average. Cost synergies could, however, largely not be reaped even three years after the merger.

II.1 Introduction

II.1.1 Objective and Motivation

For a number of years now, the German banking industry has found itself in a sustainable phase of profound consolidation. Since the reunification of East and West Germany in 1989, the number of credit institutions has more than halved from 4,500 to almost 2,200. But in comparison to its European neighbors, Germany is still considered as perhaps the most over-banked country with a high branch density.[17] The still-below average level of concentration in the industry and the therewith supposed lower degree of efficiency is primarily attributed to the high state participation and the enduring fragmentation of the German banking industry in three legally confined pillars: Private banks, cooperative banks,

---

17 Cf. Williams/Thurm (2004), p. 28, and DIW (2004), p. 31.

and the public sector.[18] Consolidation of the banking industry has occurred largely within these pillars. This is expected to continue until "in-pillar" consolidation is exhausted and banks need to look across pillars for further external growth.[19] In the period from 1993 to 2003, the number of PSBs has reduced from 703 to 489 institutions and there is evidence to suggest that the speed of consolidation will continue to accelerate.[20]

The fundamental driver behind this trend is assumed to be the crucial combination of declining returns and increasing costs,[21] which has led to a considerable deterioration of PSBs' profitability. As a result of the lasting regression of the margin of interest (which has hit PSBs particularly hard due to the high relevance of the deposit business), these institutions have strengthened their efforts to increase returns from the interest autonomous provision business. However, the buildup of competencies in business areas, which are both growth promising and interest autonomous, demands large investments in the redirection and expansion of distribution channels that can only be amortized with corresponding capacity utilization. This difficulty becomes even more problematic as regulations on banking supervision become increasingly strict and extensive; For example, the equity capital directive within Basel II requires PSBs to make considerable investments in the setup of necessary governance- and information systems.[22] Furthermore, due to the abolition of the guarantor's liability (July, 2005), PSBs have to be prepared for the incurrence of additional costs for the security fund.[23]

In light of these challenges, the German public savings banks association – Deutscher Sparkassen- und Giroverband (DSGV) – is urging its member institutions to improve their economic efficiency. German PSBs should reach a return on equity (ROE) of at least 15% and a cost-income-ratio (CIR) of at most 60% in the medium-term to remain competitive in the future.[24] For a large number of institutions, reaching these goals seems to be unachievable on their own. According to a study of A.T. Kearney (2002), only one out of ten managing directors of PSBs are convinced they are to able to achieve this on their own terms through internal restructuring measures.[25] With regard to institution spanning solutions, traditional co-operations, such as joint data processing centers and payment han-

---

18 Cf. e.g. IMF (2003), p. 33, Williams/Thurm (2004), p. 36–38, DIW (2004), p. 29, and Bundesverband Deutscher Banken (2004), p. 1.
19 Cf. Williams/Thurm (2004), p. 3.
20 Cf. Hackethal/Schmidt (2005), p. 18–20.
21 Cf. w/a (2001a), p. 19.
22 Cf. Schierenbeck/Tegeder (2004), p. 124–127.
23 Cf. DIW (2004), p. 51–54.
24 Cf. DSGV (2002), p. 12.
25 Cf. A.T. Kearney (2002), w/p.

dling organizations, have already been implemented in recent years.[26] The potential of such measures is limited, however, as the legal requirements for the outsourcing of steering- and governance processes are practically impossible and the outsourcing of market processes is only possible to a limited extent.[27] Synergies in these increasingly complex and therewith cost-intensive areas appear to be achievable only through external growth by merging different PSBs. Following the above reasoning, the consolidation trend in the public banking sector can be expected to continue. J.P. Morgan even expects that in the year 2010, there will only be around 100 PSBs left in Germany.[28]

Despite the existence of revenue- and cost synergy potential in the public banking sector, evidence on the performance of historic mergers amongst PSBs provides a negative view. In many cases, mergers amongst PSBs appeared to have a negative effect on profitability, at least in the short-term.[29] Synergies could not be reaped sufficiently. The weak performance of historic transactions seems to also have worsened public opinion: Only 15% of PSBs' managing directors believe further mergers to be a critical lever for result improvement.[30]

Accordingly, today's consolidation pressure in the public banking sector is confronted with an impression of past PSB mergers' lack of success. The present analysis wants to add evidence to this apparent conflict. For this purpose, four exemplary mergers are analyzed on a case study basis. A performance study is conducted that includes an observation period of three years before and after the merger. Findings are analyzed on a stand-alone and on an industry-related basis. Contrary to previous evidence and public opinion, results indicate that mergers amongst PSBs can indeed be successful.

II.1.2 Course of the Investigation

The course of the investigation is structured as follows: First, chapter II.2 lays out the necessary background knowledge on PSBs in Germany. Section II.2.1 provides information on the dualistic structure of the German public banking sector, followed by section II.2.2, which elaborates on the three most important characteristics of German PSBs.

Chapter II.3 then explains particularities on mergers amongst PSBs. Section II.3.1 illustrates the different possible merger types and section II.3.2 highlights

---

26 Cf. Wolfers/Kaufmann (2004), p. 209.
27 Cf. Haasis (2002), p. 30, and Wolfers/Kaufmann (2004), p. 209.
28 Cf. Ernst & Young (2003), p. 26, and w/a (2003b), w/p.
29 Cf. Haun (1996), p. 270.
30 Cf. A.T. Kearney (2002), w/p.

some legal restrictions, which are applicable in the public banking sector. Next, section II.3.3 points out possible motives to engage in a merger transaction, after which section II.3.4 identifies potential drawbacks and risks associated with such action.

Chapter II.4 then constitutes the main part of this paper as it contains the analysis. Section II.4.1 presents the limited prior research on the success of mergers amongst German PSBs. Section II.4.2 then explains the chosen methodology and provides a few "descriptive statistics" on the chosen transactions. Within section II.4.3, the individual case studies as well as the individual results are presented. Results are then put in relation to industry figures in the comparative analysis in section II.4.4.

Chapter II.5 wraps up the findings and concludes the essay.

II.2 Public Savings Banks – Structure and Attributes

To evaluate the success of mergers in the public banking sector, it is necessary to first illustrate the particularities of this sector, this pillar of the German banking industry and to clarify the restrictions to which PSBs are subject. These particularities of the public sector naturally also have an effect on the process of consolidation. Accordingly, this section provides an overview of the key constituting elements of German public savings banking (GPSB).[31] This is necessary background information to clearly interpret findings of the case study analysis on mergers within this regulated sector.

II.2.1 Organizational Structure

The organization of German public savings banking is based on a dualistic structure that regulates the division of work between PSBs and state banks. The principle of subsidiary thereby constitutes that market cultivation and customer service generally should be carried out by the first level of the structure, the PSBs. As a result, PSBs operate as universal credit institutions by providing a wide variety of banking services to private households, companies, and local authorities.[32] State banks, on the other hand, only administer those tasks that PSBs – due to legal or economic restrictions – either cannot or only inadequately carry out

---

31 The terms "public savings banking", "public banking sector", and "public sector" are used interchangeably for the corresponding German term " Sparkassensektor".
32 For this and the following cf. Weiler/Fritsch (2004), p. 218.

themselves. However, in light of substantial economic problems of individual institutions as well as essential changes in the regulatory environment, a discussion concerning the abolishment of the dualistic division of labor in the context of mergers between PSBs and state banks is growing in intensity. The following analysis, however, excludes considerations of this type of merger completely.

II.2.2 Attributes of Public Savings Banks

The constituting attributes of a PSB derive from its legal definition. According to this definition, a PSB is an absolutely safe institution of public law that has legal capacity; as a municipal firm, it must fulfill legally limited, socially binding tasks. Its liabilities are fully guaranteed by the municipal guarantor (Gewährträger).[33] This definition implies two fundamental principles of German public savings banking: Municipal obligation and public mandate.

II.2.2.1 Municipal Obligation

As an institution of public law, every PSB has an institution bearer (Anstaltsträger) which needs to be a municipal body according to savings bank legislation of the federate states.[34] According to state bank legislation, institution bearers are also called municipal guarantors as they must fully guarantee all liabilities of the PSB.[35] They appoint the member of the controlling body and the administrative board and also decide on existential changes within the bank, which includes decision on mergers with other institutions.[36] As a result of this organizational structure, municipal politics have a significant influence on market concentration within the public banking sector. Whereas the board of directors has sole responsibility of day-to-day operations, it underlies the policy-making power of the administrative board, which makes final decisions.[37]

II.2.2.2 Business Policy and Public Mandate

Savings bank legislation defines the main business purpose of a PSB oriented at the public mandate of its services, which in particular includes the guarantee and provision of banking services. According to this, a PSB is obligated to provide

---

33 Cf. Schlierbach (1998), p. 25.
34 Cf. Geiger (1992), p. 24, and Schlierbach (1998), p. 26.
35 Cf. Schlierbach (1998), p. 26.
36 Cf. Geiger (1992), p. 24.
37 Cf. Trosky (1996), p. 98–99.

residents as well as enterprises within its bearer's municipality with a both qualitatively and quantitatively sufficient offering of banking services.[38] Concurrent with the regional principle, PSBs are generally allowed to establish branches in the districts of the municipal guarantor(s), only.[39] As a result, the regional principle clearly limits the potential for organic growth and narrows alternatives for PSBs to eliminate structural differences either through co-operations or mergers with other PSBs.[40] Critics view the regional principle as one main obstacle for an effective consolidation process.[41] As a result, other European countries such as Austria, Italy and Spain, have abolished the regional principle.[42] Deriving from the provision mandate, the general purpose of PSBs to benefit the public is another constituting attribute. Making a profit is thus the only necessary condition for PSBs to be able to fulfill the primary business objective (which derives its orientation from the public mandate). PSBs are therefore primarily mandate and only indirectly profit oriented.

II.2.2.3 Public Liability

The liability regime of PSBs has been an important factor in the previous consolidation of the sector and needs to be considered in the evaluation of implemented mergers. The regime was traditionally marked by maintenance obligation (Anstaltslast) and municipal guarantor liability (Gewährträgerhaftung). In this framework, maintenance obligation refers to the liability of the bearer municipality towards the PSB, whereas municipal guarantor liability refers to the liability towards outside creditors.[43]

According to the concept of maintenance obligation, the institution bearer has the responsibility to keep the institution in due form so that it is able to fulfill its duties as long as the institution bearer pursues it.[44] As a result, the municipality as the institution bearer is obligated to offset any imminent adverse balance in order to keep the PSB operating even in a financial crisis. The magnitude of the other concept, municipal guarantor liability, is uniformly determined: The municipal guarantor is liable without restraint for creditors of its PSB. However, the creditors can only call upon the guarantor, once they cannot be satisfied out of

---

38 Cf. Dagott (2002), p. 47.
39 Cf. Geiger (1992), p. 26, and Wolfers/Kaufmann (2004), p. 208.
40 Cf. Kositzki (2004), p. 17, and Wolfers/Kaufmann (2004), p. 208.
41 Cf. IMF (2003), p. 20.
42 Cf. DIW (2004), p. 66–71.
43 Cf. Büschgen (1998), p. 89.
44 Cf. Schlierbach (1998), p. 142.

the assets of the PSB.[45] In case the PSB has more than one guarantor, e.g. after a merger, each guarantor is jointly and separately liable. The internal liability allocation between the guarantors then usually corresponds with the distribution key of profits.

After the Banking Association of the European Union had filed a complaint, the European Commission tested maintenance obligation and municipal guarantor liability for the German public banking sector. It had come to the conclusion that both are incompatible with the principles of a common market. As a result, both maintenance obligation and municipal guarantor liability were abolished in July 2001 (coming into effect on July 19th, 2005).[46] Since then, municipal bearers must act as if they were private owners. Balancing out an adverse balance is still possible, but now it requires prior approval. As a consequence, PSBs are expected to increasingly turn towards profit-oriented strategies to become more profitable and thereby more robust and independent. During this process, many PSBs will decide to enhance performance through external growth strategies, which will lead to a further increase in consolidation pressure in the public banking sector.[47] Due to the regional principle, engaging a merger is generally the only way for PSBs to significantly grow in size. On their own, PSBs are generally limited to their district (according to the regional principle).[48]

II.3 Particularities of Mergers of Public Savings Banks

II.3.1 Possible Merger Types

On the basis of the mode of a merger, it is possible to distinguish between compulsory and voluntary combinations. As compulsory mergers can only rarely be witnessed, the remainder of the analysis focuses solely on voluntary mergers. These can be further distinguished between combination through absorption and combination through new formation.[49] These two types correspond to the merger through absorption and the merger through new formation of German stock corporation law.[50] Within the concept of combination through absorption, one PSB merges into the absorbing PSB. Usually, the smaller, economically weaker PSB gives up its economic and legal entity by merging its assets with the absorbing

---

45 Cf. Schlierbach (1998), p. 137–138.
46 Cf. DIW (2004), p. 20–22.
47 Cf. Ernst & Young (2003), p. 25.
48 Cf. Williams/Thurm (2004), p. 28.
49 Cf. Wolfers/Kaufmann (2004), p. 211, and Schlierbach (1998), p. 74.
50 Cf. Bosse (1982), p. 45.

PSB.[51] The probability of this type of merger increases with the critical state of the smaller PSB and its municipal guarantor. Within the combination through new formation, a new PSB, a new entity, is established in which two or more involved PSBs merge.[52]

However, the decision on the type of combination also depends on other specific general conditions of the merger. In addition to the fiscal relevance of the type of combination, the political elements particularly need to be considered, as the municipal guarantors are the final decision makers. They could have diverging political interests. Concerning fiscal implications, a combination through absorption seems favorable, as merely the assets of the absorbed PSB need to be transferred. Amongst political considerations, however, a combination through absorption is less favorable, as the releasing municipality is losing its previous influence.[53] In addition to losing influence, considerations regarding the political appearance have historically led to a preference for a combination through new formation, particularly in the case of mergers between two PSBs of similar size.[54]

The decision-making authority regarding a merger between PSBs lies with their municipal guarantors. All savings bank legislations demand, however, that before reaching a final decision, the administrative boards of all involved PSBs need to be heard. In some federal states it is, moreover, a requirement to listen to the managing directors of the involved PSBs as well as to representatives of the applicable regional savings bank association.[55] Besides the necessity to fulfill these hearing requirements, a PSB merger also requires government approval.

II.3.2 Legal Restrictions

In some German states, savings bank legislation requires merging PSBs to be adjacent, i.e. the districts of the municipal guarantors need to adjoin.[56] Otherwise an envisaged combination cannot go through. However, these legislations have been amended in a few German states, allowing the combination of non-adjacent PSBs in which the economic and spacious proximity lead to an appropriate appearance of the merger.[57] These types of transactions are also referred to as "jump merg-

---

51 Cf. Süchting (1999), p. 95.
52 Cf. Wolfers/Kaufmann (2004), p. 211, and Bosse (1982), p. 53–66.
53 Cf. Süchting (1999), p. 96.
54 Cf. Bosse (1982), p. 50.
55 Cf. Schlierbach (1998), p. 75, Bales (1993), p. 520, and Polewsky (1994), p. 120.
56 Cf. Bosse (1982), p. 58–59.
57 Cf. §32 Abs. 1 SpkG NRW.

ers" (Sprungfusionen).[58] An adjacent location is the only prerequisite for the combination of PSBs (which is explicitly phrased in savings bank legislation). However, a merger can also be regarded as illegal if it is assumed to possibly breach fundamental organizing principles of PSBs, in particular the principles of subsidiary or region.[59]

II.3.3 Merger Motives

A large number of motives for mergers of banking institutions have been discussed in the literature.[60] The synergy hypothesis seems to be of particular importance. The reasoning is as follows: Due to cost pressures within the public banking sector and the necessity, as proclaimed by the DSGV, that PSBs in Germany need to improve ROE- and CIR performance,[61] PSBs have had to restructure their operations. As internal restructuring options are usually limited, needed performance improvements can often not be achieved alone. The considerable merger activity amongst PSBs, which could be observed in the last two decades,[62] implies that many PSBs have merged with other institutions in order to increase performance. Reaping synergies in both cost and revenue terms by combining two (and sometimes more) banking institutions to improve performance and increase value can be subsumed under the synergy hypothesis.[63] Recent evidence confirms the predominance of the synergy hypothesis. The primary objective of most banking mergers is to increase performance through reaping synergies.[64] This also appears to be applicable for PSB combinations.[65]

Cost synergies can be reaped by exploiting economies of scale. In the private banking sector, the largest synergy potential is generally perceived to be a reduction in the number of branches enabled through overlapping branch structures.[66] Due to the regional principle, PSB mergers rarely feature branch overlaps. As a result, synergies within combinations of PSBs mainly need to be reaped through

---

58 Cf. Bentele (2003), p. 17. A recent example for this type of transaction is the merger between Stadtsparkasse Köln and Sparkasse Bonn. Cf. w/a (2004c), p. 17.
59 Cf. Bosse (1982), p. 60.
60 For an overview cf. e.g. Beitel (2002), p. 13–30, Tröger (2003), p. 61–234, and Walter (2004), p. 60–98.
61 Cf. DSGV (2002), p. 12.
62 Cf. Hackethal/Schmidt (2005), p. 18–20.
63 Cf. Beitel (2002), p. 18.
64 Cf. Bremke et al. (2004), p. 4.
65 Cf. Sauer (2004), p. 170, and Kienbaum Management Consultants (2002), p. 21.
66 Cf. The Boston Consulting Group (2004), p. 8–10.

the integration of back office operations and administrative functions.[67] Making the situation even more difficult, administrative boards are generally very restrictive concerning the approval of restructuring measures, particularly in regard to reduction of staff. Reductions in personnel costs normally can be achieved gradually through partial retirement and no new hires.[68]

But synergies can also be reaped on the revenue side. Particularly the exploitation of economies of scope, for which the existing distribution channels are consolidated and product portfolios are bundled, lead to revenue increases at the merged PSB (and possibly to decreasing relative costs as well).[69] Product cross-selling potential can also be utilized. Finally, a higher specialization level of the sales and distribution force can be attained.

Synergies can additionally be reaped on the financial side through the combination of credit portfolios. If the cash flows (and the according risks) of the individual credit portfolios are weakly correlated, the combination of those credit portfolios diversifies and thereby improves the overall risk position.[70] This is particularly applicable for PSB mergers, as due to the regional principle, a combination and diversification of credit portfolios is only possible through the combination of different PSBs.[71] Additionally, mergers can have balancing effects on the combined equity so that judicially defined credit size limits are broadened[72] – especially in the merger of PSBs with different balance sheet structures.[73]

Another motive for a merger between PSBs could be that one institution is in financial distress. Within such a distress merger, another PSB would jump in and merge with the weakened one.[74] In the public banking sector, a distress merger is generally preferred over the bankruptcy of a PSB.[75] One reason could be that rescuing another distressed PSB by merging operations can result in considerable tax advantages. As the PSB in financial distress will have usually accumulated significant tax losses, these can be carried forward and utilized by the other PSB against its profit to alleviate or even eliminate the tax burden for the current and possibly subsequent years.[76]

---

67 Cf. Schäfer (2004), p. 180, Haasis (2002), p. 28, and Sauer (2004), p. 171.
68 Cf. w/a (2004a), p. 22.
69 For this paragraph cf. Schäfer (2004), p. 179–180.
70 Cf. Sauer (2004), p. 172.
71 Cf. Gerke (2004), p. 36.
72 Cf. Schnatterer (1994), p. 74–75.
73 Cf. Haun (1996), p. 36, and w/a (2005), p. 4.
74 Cf. Haun (1996), p. 253, and Elsas (2004), p. 1. The merger between Sparkasse Mannheim and Sparkasse Weinheim covered in the second case study is a good example of a distress merger (section II.4.3.2.).
75 Cf. Hackethal (2003), p. 10.
76 Case study two illustrates the tax-loss carry forward motive (section II.4.3.2.).

Finally, it is worth remembering that any decision to merge two (or more) PSBs is made by the municipal guarantor. Therefore it is possible that the decision to merge different PSBs can be driven by political rather than economic motives.

II.3.4 Possible Drawbacks and Risks

Although mergers are generally intended to yield benefits, there are also possible drawbacks and risks which need to be considered. Costs for integrating the formerly separate institutions, e.g. for the combination of information technology (IT), external consultants or reconstruction measures, can be large.[77] Besides one-time restructuring costs, there is the danger of costs remaining on a high level. Within the public banking sector, the loss of local attachment is seen as the most critical risk in this respect, as consolidation continues and PSBs become larger, with coverage often spanning multiple municipalities. The traditional regional focus that has led to distinct proximity to customers, personal client relationships, and a quick response to local market demands is considered to be at risk.[78] Less personal client relationships do not necessarily lead to the loss of the customer, but this development does increase clients' price sensitivity and willingness to switch banks.[79]

Further possible risks of merging two or more banking operations can be seen in increased complexity and coordination requirements[80] as well as in differences in salary structures and retirement schemes.[81] Increased complexity and coordination requirements are expected to result in cost increases. Similarly differences in salary structures are generally balanced out upwards, which thereby is expected to lead to an increase in personnel costs.

As PSB mergers often had an adverse effect on short-term profitability, both prior research and public opinion have had a rather negative view on this type of transaction. It seems that oftentimes synergy potential has not been fully exploited and/or integration costs and risk had been underestimated.

---

77 Cf. Sauer (2004), p. 172, Becker (1997), p. 176–181, and w/a (2005), p. 4.
78 Cf. Süchting (1999), p. 89.
79 Cf. Becker (1997), p. 190. This risk is sometimes considered more important than the abolition of the municipal guarantor liability, cf. w/a (2004a), p. 22.
80 Cf. Paul (2004), p. 307.
81 Cf. Becker (1997), p. 190.

II.4 Analysis of Merger Success

II.4.1 Prior Research

Two prior studies analyze the success of German PSB mergers.[82] They both come to a negative overall assessment of PSB mergers. Haun (1996) analyzes the performance of all 24 mergers between West German PSBs in the period from 1979 to 1988.[83] A key finding of the study is that mergers between PSBs lead to significant performance deterioration at the combined entity. This effect is understood to be mainly due to considerable increases in administrative costs, which more than compensate a possible positive effect on revenues. Results of the study differ, however, in relation to pre-merger performance. PSBs that have underperformed the sector average and engage in merger activities can generally expect positive performance developments. On the contrary, PSBs that have outperformed the sector average before the merger usually exhibit below average performance progression in the merger process. In this case, anticipated positive effects from growth cannot be fully captured due to already existing substantial growth.

Gold (1997) finds similar though less significant evidence in the analysis of 31 PSB mergers that occurred between 1972 and 1979.[84] Results indicate that administrative costs, on average, decrease with time delay. More importantly, however, findings point towards a slump in the PSBs ROE after the merger, which could also be due to valuation measures undertaken in the process. Unfortunately, the study is unable to determine key drivers that decide on the success of a PSB merger.

Due to the structural similarity of PSBs and credit unions (Genossenschaftsbanken), the study of Terbroke (1993) needs to be mentioned.[85] The analysis of 154 mergers of German credit unions in the period from 1983 to 1985 concluded with a negative assessment. Nevertheless, around 40% of the analyzed banks can reap as many anticipated synergies in the first three years following the merger so that negative effects from the merger are balanced out and a positive effect for the combined entity is achieved.

To conclude, the limited prior research on PSB mergers comes to a negative assessment, particularly on short-term effects of both costs and profitability. In the medium-term, mergers could possibly become value creating, as PSBs need

---

82 Cf. Haun (1996) and Gold (1997).
83 Cf. Haun (1996).
84 Cf. Gold (1997).
85 Cf. Tebroke (1993).

38

comparably longer to capture synergies. Finally, restructuring seems to generally only be able to be achieved on a gradual basis, particularly in the area of personnel costs.

II.4.2 Methodology

II.4.2.1 Study Design

There are generally three different approaches on how to assess the success of mergers: Capital market oriented event study, performance study, and dynamic efficiency study.[86] Since PSBs are not publicly listed and therefore have no readily observable market price, the event study approach, which relies on share price data, is not suitable to analyze PSB mergers. In accordance with prior research of Haun (1996) and Gold (1997), the following analysis is applying performance study methodology.[87] The success of a merger can thereby be evaluated by calculating selected performance figures which are derived from annual accounts of the involved PSBs. These performance figures are calculated for a specified observation period before and after the merger. Whereas it is usually assumed that 85% of the anticipated synergies are reaped in the first year, German banks are slower and need, on average, about two years for this achievement.[88] PSB mergers are assumed to need an even longer period of three years to reap these synergies.[89] Accordingly, this study applies an observation period (which includes annual accounts) from three years before to three years after the merger. For example, for a merger involving two PSBs, the case study analysis would usually incorporate ten annual accounts (three accounts each prior to the merger and four accounts of the combined entity).

II.4.2.2 Merger Selection

Selected mergers had to be completed at least three to four years prior to the analysis, as the observation period includes annual accounts of up to three years after the merger. In light of this situation, selected mergers must have occurred before January 2003.

---

86 For an overview of the three different approaches cf. Beitel/Schiereck (2003), p. 502–506.
87 Cf. Haun (1996) and Gold (1997).
88 Cf. Röckemann/Schiereck (2004), p. 4.
89 Cf. Baxmann (1995), p. 393, and w/a (2005), p. 4.

To provide a more interesting analysis, the chosen transactions resemble the following four quite different ideal types of PSB mergers:
- Combination through absorption between a large and a small PSB.
- Distress merger of two similar PSBs.
- "Normal" combination of two adjacent PSBs.
- Combination of multiple PSBs across regional boundaries.

Table II.1 presents the four mergers which were selected for the analysis. The legally absorbing institute is marked in italics. Three mergers occurred in the year 2000 and one transaction was announced in 1996. Absorbed total assets range from around €350 million in the merger of a large and a small PSB (case 1) to €3.5 billion in the combination of multiple PSBs (case 4). Each merger is discussed in detail in the case study analysis in section II.4.3.

Table II.1: Overview of Selected Mergers

No.	Name Post-Merger	Names Pre-Merger *	Year of Merger	Absorbed Total Assets (in EUR)
1	SK Coesfeld	– *SK Coesfeld* – SSK Dülmen	1996	714 million**
2	SK Rhein Neckar Nord	SK Mannheim *SK Weinheim*	2000	2.69 billion
3	SK Bamberg	*SK Bamberg* KSK Bamberg	2000	1.64 billion
4	SK Mainfranken Würzburg	SK Main-Spessart KuSSK Kitzingen KSK Würzburg-Ochsenfurt *SK Würzburg*	2000	3.50 billion

* Absorbing institute marked in italics.
** Denominated in Deutsche Mark.
Source: Annual reports.

According to an observation period of seven years spanning three years before and after the merger[−3;3], annual accounts of all prior PSBs are analyzed for the pre-merger period [−3;−1]. To cover the year of the merger {0} as well as the post-merger period [1;3], annual accounts of the combined entity for these years are considered. Overall, 46 annual accounts are included in the performance study of the four transactions. In addition, results are put in relation to the sector average to allow for a more meaningful interpretation of the evidence. For this purpose, consolidated balance sheet and income statement data of the German public banking sector (excluding state banks), which was provided by the Bundesbank,, is utilized. To get the desired performance ratios, the consolidation of individual balance sheet and income statement figures is carried out in accordance with the scheme proposed by the Bundesbank.[90] This process ensures data consistence, as transaction data of the four mergers is calculated in accordance with the Bundesbank scheme as well.

II.4.2.3 Performance Indicators

The performance of a PSB can be measured with a few common success oriented key figures.[91] To ensure consistency and clarity of the analyzed performance figures, a hierarchical performance measurement system is applied. The top performance figure of this hierarchical system is ROE, as banks both in the private and the public sector employ ROE as the main performance indicator and control figure.[92] It seems that such a relative performance measure is more meaningful than absolute figures as it, amongst other things, allows the direct comparison of results of different banks. In this approach, different cost or revenue positions are always put into relation to the size of the business, such as total assets. Accordingly, the following case study analysis focuses solely on relative performance measurement to assess the success of mergers in the public banking sector.

II.4.3 Stand-Alone Case Study Analysis

The case study analysis within this section consists of two steps for each merger. In the first step, details on the transactions are laid out. This includes an illustration of background information and motives behind the merger. In the second step, the development of performance measures, such as ROE and CIR, as well as individual profit and loss account figures that drive the observed development, are presented. In this section, calculations are first carried out on a stand-alone basis of the merger to better isolate individual effects. Results of the performance analysis in relation to sector averages are then presented in section II.4.4.

---

90 Cf. Deutsche Bundesbank (2004), p. 34–35.
91 Cf. Appendix I for a definition of the performance figures applied in this study. For an overview also cf. Schierenbeck (1994), p. 334–338.
92 Cf. Fischer/Lanz (2004), p. 364, and DSGV (2002), p. 12.

II.4.3.1 Case Study One – Large absorbs Small

Background Information

In the beginning of 1996, Sparkasse Coesfeld and Stadtsparkasse Dülmen merged their operations. The transaction was structured as a combination through absorption in which the much larger Sparkasse Coesfeld (almost four times larger in terms of total assets) absorbed the Stadtsparkasse Dülmen. Sparkasse Coesfeld has a rather vivid merger history. Originally, Sparkasse Coesfeld resulted from the merger between three PSBs, namely the Kreissparkasse Lüdinghausen, Stadtsparkasse Coesfeld, and Kreissparkasse Coesfeld that occurred in 1978.[93] After the merger with Stadtsparkasse Dülmen, which is analyzed here, it absorbed another PSB with the Stadtsparkasse Billerbeck in 2002. Most recently, Sparkasse Coesfeld merged with Kreissparkasse Borken to form the Sparkasse West-münsterland, which now covers multiple municipalities and rural regions.

The motives for the merger were straightforward:[94] The combination was intended to result in the formation of the largest credit institution within the district, which was expected to increase performance and service capability. Its aim was to improve the position of the Sparkasse Coesfeld and thereby strengthen its ability to fulfill the public mandate. A key element of the merger process was the integration of procedures and organizational setup as well as the consolidation of IT structures and systems.[95] To support the integration efforts, a total of eight task forces were formed according to functional area with equal representation of the merging PSBs. The total list of tasks amounted to 400 individual positions which were all carried out until the end of the merger year. Integration was finally completed with the linking of both data processing centers in the beginning of November 1996. In addition to these integration activities, Sparkasse Coesfeld also refurbished one branch and opened two new ones in 1996 in rural districts.[96] Significant lay-offs were not envisaged within the transaction. The number of employees remained steady at around 630[97] (including all 20 apprentices).

---

93 Cf. Sparkasse Westmünsterland (2006), w/p, for the merger history of the Sparkasse Westmünsterland.
94 Cf. Sparkasse Coesfeld (1996), p. 6.
95 Cf. Sparkasse Coesfeld (1996), p. 8.
96 Cf. Sparkasse Coesfled (1996), p. 8.
97 Cf. Sparkasse Coesfeld (1996), p. 9.

Analysis of Merger Success

At first glance, the stand-alone analysis of merger success provides a negative view of the combination: ROE drops from 21.5% in the pre-merger period to 16.6% in the post-merger period and CIR increases from 60.1% to 67.6% over the same interval. This development is, however, partly driven by a large one-time increase in administration costs in 1998. Nevertheless, considerable operational synergies do not seem to have been realized. The analysis of applicable income statement positions and their development, as illustrated in figure II.1, provides a more detailed view. It shows the individual profit and loss account ratios which have driven the development of the net profit margin. An increase in a profit margin benefits net profit, whereas an increase in a cost margin has a negative effect on the net profit margin.

Figure II.1: Net Profit Margin Development Pre- to Post Merger (Case 1)

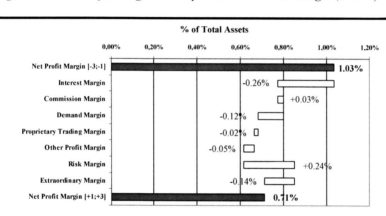

Source: Personal calculations; data: Annual reports.

First of all, figure II.1 shows that the net profit margin amounted to an average of 1.03% in the three years before the merger and decreased to a level of 0.71% post-merger. This development is, however, largely driven by non-operational cost figures in the equivalent post merger period. The interest margin, which largely depends on the market environment, [98] deteriorates significantly by

---

98 The analysis within section II.4.4. provides results in relation to industry averages and thereby allows better identification and interpretation of merger-related changes in performance, which are not due to market factors.

0.26%. To make things worse, the extraordinary margin falls by 0.14%. Taken together, a negative effect of 0.4% derives from market or extraordinary factors. On the contrary, it is interesting that the risk margin halves itself by 0.24%, thereby having the largest single positive change effect on results. Possibly, the merging of different credit portfolios leads to risk diversification and an improvement of the overall risk position. Another positive development that should be mentioned is the increase in the commission margin of 0.03%. The 0.12% increase in the demand margin (Bedarfsspanne) needs to be viewed critically, however, as it is here that operational synergies could have been achieved, but conversely, costs increased. But as lay-offs were not a proclaimed post-merger strategy, a significant improvement in the demand margin could not be expected.

To conclude, the merger did not yield significant benefits for the combining PSBs on a stand-alone basis. However, results are largely driven by the deterioration of the interest margin, which should be mainly attributable to outside market factors and high extraordinary costs. Neglecting these figures would result in a positive assessment of the transaction. The improved risk position and the increased commission margin particularly highlight the success of a merger. The significant increase in the demand margin should be viewed carefully, however.

II.4.3.2 Case Study Two – Distress Merger

Background Information

The merger of Sparkasse Mannheim and Bezirkssparkasse Weinheim formed the new Sparkasse Rhein Neckar Nord in December 2000. This combination can be considered as a typical distress merger. At the end of the 1990s, a careless credit allocation, amongst other things, had forced Sparkasse Mannheim into a particularly difficult financial situation. Until the end of 1998, a total of €400 million in write-offs had to be accounted for in its books.[99] As a result of this financial disaster, the city of Mannheim had to inject €25 million in cash and needed to provide recoverability guarantees for capital in the amount of €75 million. The regional PSB association provided cash allowances of another €75 million and the DSGV assigned an interest free loan to be used as additional surplus. The Sparkasse Mannheim crisis was the most expensive restructuring case in Germany's public banking sector.[100]

Motives for the merger need to be viewed in light of the different situation each of the merging PSBs was in before the merger took place. On one side, Be-

---

99 Cf. w/a (2001c), p. 24.
100 Cf. w/a (2003a), p. 18.

zirkssparkasse Weinheim considered itself as too small and wanted to grow externally through the combination; it feared that market demands in growth areas could not be fully satisfied in the future without this merger. The merger was intended to deliver considerable cost synergies as well as an increase in market power, which would ultimately result in raised profitability for the combined entity.[101] But another central motive for the merger was to utilize the huge tax loss carry-forwards that Sparkasse Mannheim had accumulated due to financial distress, and to do so before the tax legislation reform came into effect in 2001.[102] Possible tax savings were estimated to amount to more than €25 million.[103] The tax effect was intended to thereby rehabilitate the balance sheet through increases in equity.[104] In addition, it was hoped for an improvement in the overall risk position as the combination of the different credit portfolios should lead to better diversification.[105] In contrast to other mergers, it seems that operational restructuring was not the main objective in this transaction. Despite the critical financial situation Sparkasse Mannheim had found itself in before the merger took place, it was agreed by both sides that no operational lay-offs shall be made. It was merely planned to undertake an analysis on the future personnel structure of the combined entity.[106]

Analysis of Merger Success

As expected, the ROE was negative at –18.1% in the pre-merger period due to the adverse financial situation of Sparkasse Mannheim. It seems that the merger was successful, as ROE was turned around to a level of 3.9% after the merger. This improvement mainly stems from the normalization of the risk margin, which was particularly high due to the distressed financial situation in the year before the merger in which the largest part of the write-offs needed to be made. The CIR, however, develops unfavorable as it increases from 74.6% to 83.5%. Operational synergies were not a cited merger motive and could not be reaped. Instead, costs even seem to have increased.

As expected in a distress merger, the net profit margin is clearly negative in the pre-merger period at –0.83%. The enhancement of the risk margin is of course very large in this case. It amounts to 1.57% (!). However, this drastic posi-

---

101 Cf. w/a (2001b), p. 110.
102 Accumulated tax losses of €90 million could be theoretically offset against earnings of the Bezirkssparkasse Weinheim.
103 Cf. w/a (2001b), p. 110.
104 Cf. w/a (2000b), p. 9.
105 Cf. Elsas (2004), p. 2.
106 Cf. w/a (2001c), p. 24.

tive change is partly cushioned by a deterioration of the interest margin. Although temporarily more than 50 employees (almost 5% of total staff) were involved in the integration efforts,[107] personnel costs were slightly reduced after the merger. In combination with small improvements in the demand margin, it seems that some synergies could be reaped on both technical and organizational levels. Commission and proprietary trading margins remained fairly stable. Overall, the efficiency increase in the administration is too small to compensate for the deterioration of the interest margin. As personnel restructurings were not planned and thus not realized, the witnessed normalization of overall results points towards a positive assessment on the success of this distress merger.

Figure II.2 shows the development of the net profit margin and the individual margins driving this development in the second case study.

Figure II.2: Net Profit Margin Development Pre- to Post Merger (Case 2)

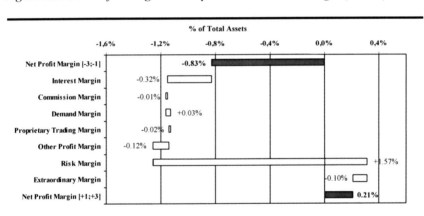

Source: Personal calculations; data: Annual reports.

II.4.3.3 Case Study Three – "Normal" Merger

Background Information

The merger of SK Bamberg and KSK Bamberg in July 2000 formed one of the largest PSBs in Bavaria, with total assets of €2.84 million and more than 900 employees for the combined entity. The new municipal guarantor was a special

---

107   Cf. w/a (2004b), p. 470.

purpose vehicle (SPV) that was backed by the city of Bamberg as well as by the rural district. Due to tax considerations, the merger was structured as a combination through absorption in which the SK Bamberg represented the absorbing institute.[108] The transaction was supposed to allow achieving cost synergies through efficiency increases in back office operations. Consolidating staff and service functions should result in economies of scale. Management also hoped for improvements on the revenue side through an increase of commission business as a result of better customer relationship management.[109] Combining distribution channels and product portfolios of the two PSBs could lead to economies of scope. For the protection of customer interests during the merger process, side conditions aimed at increasing the provision of credit services to the local economy and at the achievement of a favorable pricing structure for private client accounts.[110] This again underlines the orientation of the public mandate of PSBs.

Analysis of Merger Success

The stand-alone comparison of pre and post-merger ROE and CIR figures yields a rather negative impression of the transaction. Whereas ROE was on a solid level of 21.9% before the merger, it considerable deteriorates to 8.6% after the merger. Over the same period, CIR increases from 67.1% to a level of 68.5%. Relative costs have thus slightly increased during the merger process. As figure II.3 shows, the net profit margin falls from 0.83% in the pre-merger period to 0.36% after the merger. The decrease in profitability is mainly due to a large increase in the risk margin. The negative unexpected development of the risk margin more than halves the net profit margin by 0.52% to a level of 0.36%. Interest and commission margins improve, which is, however, more than offset by an even larger rise of the demand margin. These costs are probably linked to high investments in IT and distribution channels, which the SK Bamberg viewed as a necessary condition for the merger to achieve an increase in market share.[111]

As figure II.3 shows, personnel costs again increase and are probably linked to the equalization of employee pay structures. The number of employees has not been reduced in the merger process, but instead rose slightly. However, employment exhibits a structural change from full- to part-time. Accordingly, it will take additional time for considerable personnel cost reductions to appear in the accounts.

---

108   Cf. Sparkasse Bamberg (2000), p. 3.
109   Cf. Kreissparkasse Bamberg (2000), p. 11, and Sparkasse Bamberg (2000), p. 19.
110   Cf. Sparkasse Bamberg (2001), p. 11.
111   Cf. Sparkasse Bamberg (2002), p. 11.

Figure II.3: Net Profit Margin Development Pre- to Post Merger (Case 3)

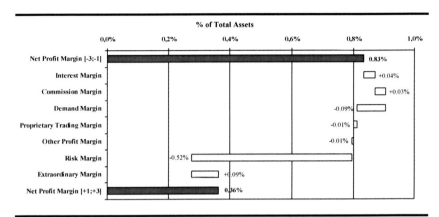

Source: Personal calculations; data: Annual reports.

II.4.3.4 Case Study Four – Multiple PSB Merger

Background Information

On January 1st, 2000, four PSBs, namely Kreissparkasse Würzburg-Ochsenfurt (KSK), Sparkasse Main-Spessart (SK), Stadtsparkasse Würzburg (SSK), and Kreis- und Stadtsparkasse Kitzingen (KuSSK), merged to form Sparkasse Main-franken-Würzburg. In the year of the merger, the combined entity had total assets amounting to around €5.8 billion and a personnel headcount of 1,796 employees. The new entity thereby became the second largest PSB in the state Bavaria and positioned itself under the top 5% of the largest PSBs in Germany.[112] This merger, which spanned several rural districts, was a novelty for public banking in Bavaria, as until then the policy of "one bank – one district" had been applied.[113] The objective of the merger was to reap sustainable cost synergies in back office operations and to achieve additional profitability improvements as a result of superior specialization of individual business units (in particular, insurance and real estate).[114] Any synergy effects, however, were expected to result not only in performance improvements. As a result of equalizing the different pricing systems of

---

112 Cf. w/a (2000a), p. 56.
113 Cf. Huebner (1999), w/p.
114 Cf. Sparkasse Mainfranken Würzburg (2001), p. 15.

the four banks, a price advantage for private clients of around €1 million per year was estimated to develop.

Analysis of Merger Success

ROE was at a solid 15.6% during the pre-merger period. Within the merger process it then decreased to 8.3% in the post-merger period. CIR was close to the 60% proclaimed by the DSGV, but rose significantly to 72.7% after the merger. Again, relative costs increased during the merger process and cost synergies could not be reaped sufficiently. Accordingly, the net profit margin fell from 0.87% to 0.52% over the same interval. It appears that the deterioration of the interest margin (of 0.31%) is the largest negative driver of the decreasing net profit margin. As interest margins usually mainly depend on the general market environment, it remains questionable whether the deterioration of the interest margin is merger related. Despite hoped-for synergy potential that was supposed to be reaped in the insurance and real estate business units, the corresponding commission margin increased by only 0.01%.

Figure II.4: Net Profit Margin Development Pre- to Post Merger (Case 4)

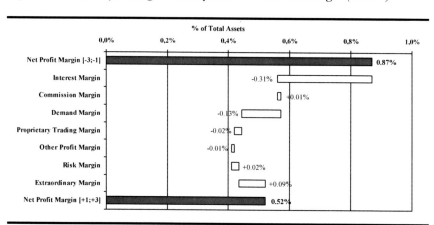

Source: Personal calculations; data: Annual reports.

The second largest change driver is the demand margin that worsens the net profit margin by 0.13%. This can supposedly be attributed to large IT integration costs, which temporarily occupied a few hundred employees as well as external consultants.[115] However, the steady rise of the demand margin until even three years after the merger can not be solely attributed to one-time restructuring activities. It rather seems that the objective of a gentle merger, which was stressed by the executive board, has resulted in a lasting increase in personnel costs. To avoid resistance of the employees, the idea to quickly restructure the organization and realize cost synergies had been abandoned and the number of employees in administrative division even increased.[116] Not until the third post-merger year did the PSB start to discuss personnel measures, which however were to be carried out without layoffs through natural employee fluctuation.[117] In addition to the rise in personnel costs, large investments in building construction, IT and software had a negative effect on results.[118]

The above figure illustrates the negative development of the CIR: Falling interest margins could neither be compensated by an increasing commission income nor cost savings in administrative functions. The impact of the operative weakness on the net profit margin was cushioned by the high valuation result and a particularly high extraordinary margin (ausserordentliche Spanne).

II.4.4 Comparative Analysis

For an investigation of results in comparison to industry averages, the stand-alone analysis of each case is put in relation to the equivalent figures of the total of all German PSBs of the time. The relative deviation from the mean is thereby calculated as follows:[119]

$$Xi_a = \frac{X_a - X_{industry}}{|X_{industry}|}$$

The relative development of merger success is analyzed according to the above formula within four intervals. The first two intervals span the three pre-merger years [-3;-1] as well as the three post-merger years [+1;+3], for which means are calculated. The other two values resemble the ration of the year of the merger [0] as well as the ratio of the third year after the merger [+3].

---

115 Cf. Sparkasse Mainfranken Würzburg (2001), p. 15.
116 Cf. Schimmer (2003), p. 23.
117 Cf. Sparkasse Mainfranken Würzburg (2004), p. 44.
118 Cf. Sparkasse Mainfranken Würzburg (2001), p. 29.
119 Cf. Haun (1996), p. 104.

The comparative analysis starts with the most important top performance figure: ROE. ROE is also the main performance indicator and control figure for banks. Figure II.5 presents the relative ROE deviation for the four analyzed mergers from the industry average of the matching periods.

Figure II.5: Development of Industry-Related Return on Equity (ROE)

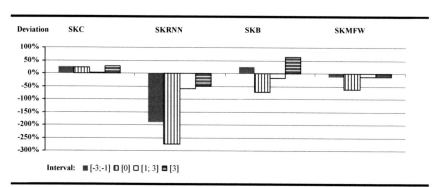

Source: Personal calculations; data: Annual reports, Bundesbank.

Within three out of the four analyzed mergers (SKRNN, SKB, and SKMFW), ROE falls within the year of the merger. Concurrent with Gold (1997), this is assumed to be stemming from one-time integration costs and valuation procedures.[120] An improvement in industry-related ROE in the third year after the merger as compared to the pre-merger period can be exhibited in three transactions (SKC, SKRNN, and SKB). ROE in the fourth merger remains unchanged. Concerning the top performance ratio, the analyzed transactions can, on average, be considered successful, as ROE generally improves.

This positive view, however, needs to be put into perspective of the development of costs. As could be seen from the individual analysis, ROE improvement is presumably not a result of operational restructuring that resulted in cost savings, but rather stems from an improvement in other areas. As figure II.6 illustrates, three out of the four mergers exhibit an enhancement in the risk margin after the combination (SKC, SKRNN, and SKMFW). Only the Bamberg merger exhibits an increase in risk. It is also noticeable that only in the distress merger balance sheet are adjustments through write-offs made, which leads to a very large deviation of the industry average risk margin in the year of the merger.

---

120   Cf. Gold (1997), p. 214.

Figure II.6: Development of Industry-Related Risk Margin

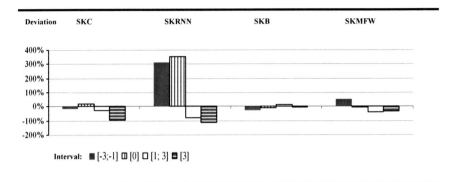

Source: Personal calculations; data: Annual reports, Bundesbank.

The development of the demand margin deserves particular attention, as it is here where cost synergies can generally be achieved. As restructuring efforts in administrative and back office functions should ultimately result in a reduction of administrative costs, this would directly result in an improvement of the demand margin. However, this could not be achieved in the analyzed cases, as figure II.7 shows below. It presents the deviation of the demand margin from the industry mean in the four analyzed mergers.

Figure II.7: Development of Industry-Related Demand Margin

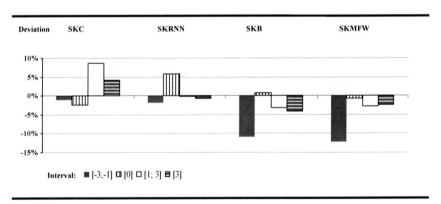

Source: Personal calculations; data: Annual reports, Bundesbank.

The demand margin generally increases in the year of the merger and afterwards. In all four cases these costs remain on a higher level in the third year after the merger as compared to the pre-transaction period. This observation is consistent with prior studies.[121] The development of the demand margin indicates that potential synergies were too small to compensate integration costs and/or that synergy potential could not be reaped fully.

The analysis of the personnel cost margin allows a more decided assessment of personnel cost development. As figure II.8 shows below, the personnel cost margin does not decrease, but rather increases during the merger process in relation to the sector average.

Figure II.8: Development of Industry-Related Personnel Cost Margin

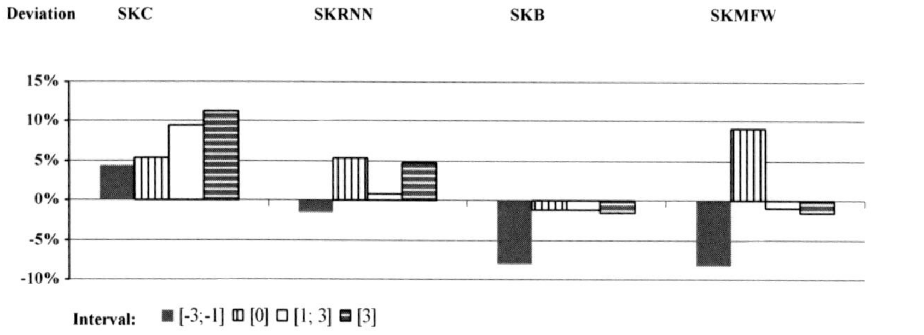

Source: Personal calculations; data: Annual reports, Bundesbank.

As expected, personnel costs increase particularly in the year of the combination. Payment structures were generally balanced out upwards, which is concurrent with findings of Gold (1997).[122] Interestingly, in all four cases, personnel costs increased after the merger. No PSB even reached the pre-merger level. Reaping some cost synergies in this area through the integration of staff divisions and back office operation could have been expected over a three year period. However, it seems that PSBs need a longer time for personnel cost improvements, as dismissals are only carried out on a socially compatible basis.

The adverse developments of the different cost margins mentioned above also have a negative effect on the top cost figure. During the merger year, an increase

---

121 Cf. Haun (1996), p. 148.
122 Cf. Gold (1997), p. 214.

in CIR can generally be witnessed in the case studies (figure II.9). However, from before to after the merger, industry-related CIR only increases in two cases and even improves in the other two. It seems that in the latter cases, improvements on the revenue side more than compensated for the cost increases in other areas and that some cost cutting potential might have been exploited as well. Figure II.9 illustrates the development of the industry-related CIR for the four analyzed transactions.

Figure II.9: Development of Industry-Related Cost Income Ratio (CIR)

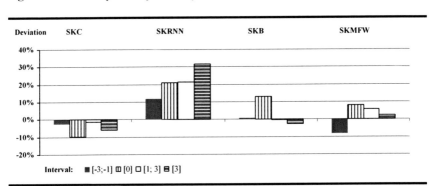

Source: Personal calculations; data: Annual reports, Bundesbank.

To conclude, the analysis of the four combinations in the public banking sector provides a mixed but overall positive view on the success of these mergers. In relation to the sector average, an improvement in ROE, which is an important measure of success, is found. The bottom line, on average, improved. This positive development is, however, contrasted with an adverse progression, particularly with personnel costs, which results in an increase in CIR in two cases. But in the other two mergers, CIR even improves against the industry mean. It appears that large parts of the cost synergies could apparently not be reaped even three years after the merger. Found improvements generally stem from advances on the revenue side through e.g. an increase in the commission margin and decreases in the risk margin due to diversification of the credit portfolio.

II.5 Conclusion

The German banking industry has been in a sustainable phase of profound consolidation for several years already. Until present, most of this restructuring occurred within and not across the German banking pillars. One pillar under particular consolidation pressure is the public banking sector, in which consolidation activity is expected to further increase. The abolishment of state guarantees (as demanded by EU ruling that came into effect in July 2005) added an additional element to the consolidation trend in the sector. The increasing consolidation pressure is, however, confronted with the broad negative assessment from both researchers and practitioners of the majority of past mergers which have proven to be rather unsuccessful.

The case-based analysis undertaken within this study adds evidence to this negative assessment of mergers in the public banking sector. Results are positive in numerous respects and demonstrate that PSB mergers can indeed be successful. Most importantly, the top performance figures applied by banks generally increases over the observation period of three years after the merger. Three of the four analyzed transactions resulted in an improvement of ROE in relation to the public sector average. However, this positive development seems to mainly stem from improvements in revenue and risk terms. Cost synergies could largely not be reaped even three years after the merger and generally rather increase during the merger process. In particular, personnel costs rise as personnel restructuring measures are very limited or non-existent. Such initiatives usually refrain from lay-offs per-se and instead rather try to reduce the workforce exclusively through natural fluctuation. In any case, reaping cost synergies appears to be difficult in PSB mergers, as costs generally increase across analyzed transactions. However, reaping cost synergies is generally not a key objective of mergers in the public banking sector. Some instead view the primary objective of PSB mergers in the achievement of synergies in revenue terms through means of strategic business reorientation.[123] This seems to have been achieved in three of the four analyzed mergers, as revenues increase more in relation to costs and thereby lead to an improvement in industry-related ROE.

It can therefore be subsumed that despite their bad reputations, PSB mergers can indeed be successful. Although costs tend to increase, improvements in other revenue generative areas more than compensate for this development and lead to an overall improvement of the bottom line. Anticipated future consolidation in the public banking sector can thus be awaited with optimistic expectations on the success of these mergers.

Regarding the measurement of merger success in the public banking sector, it seems that due to the particularities of the sector, different measurement standards need to be applied. As restructuring changes tend to take more time than in "normal" mergers, an extension of the observation period could lead to more re-

---

123   Cf. Schäfer (2004), p. 183.

liable results. This would allow capturing merger-induced performance changes that appear after more than three years.

Appendix

Commission Margin:	Commission Surplus/Average Total Assets
Cost Income Ratio (CIR):	Demand Margin/Earnings Margin
Demand Margin:	(General Administration Costs + Depreciation and Value Adjustments + Other Operational Costs)/ Average Total Assets
Earnings Margin:	Interest Margin + Commission Margin
Gross Profit Margin:	Earnings Margin – Demand Margin
Interest Margin:	Interest Surplus/Average Total Assets
Net Profit Margin:	Gross Profit Margin – Risk Margin
Personnel Margin:	Personnel Costs/Average Total Assets
Return on Equity (ROE):	Net Profit Margin/Average Equity Ratio
Risk Margin:	(Depreciation and Write-offs on Claims and Commercial Paper + Increases in Credit Provisions)/Average Total Assets

III Shareholder Wealth Effects at Rival Banks: Empirical Evidence on European Cross-Border M&A

Abstract

The European banking industry has been reshaped by an unprecedented level of consolidation activity since the early 1990s. The majority of observed M&A thereby occurred within national borders, as cross-border M&A were perceived as more difficult and costly. Moreover, regulators and governments tried to fend off foreign bidders in order to protect domestic banking markets and to create national banking champions. But are cross-border M&A really threatening the banking industry in the domestic market of entry? And do they also affect the European banking industry as a whole? The limited prior research in this area focuses exclusively on the effects on bidders and target. As a consequence, the question still remains whether cross-border M&A have negative or positive effects on the domestic (and European) banking industry as a whole.

This paper aims to fill this research gap by assessing the effects of a sample of 51 cross-border banking M&As in the European Union from 1990 to 2005 on bidders, targets, and a large set of European rivals.

Findings indicate large positive and significant returns for target shareholders, small insignificant returns for bidder shareholders, and on average, a positive effect for the combined entity. Most importantly, effects on European rival banks are found to be positive and significant. This positive effect grows with proximity to the target and is largest in the domestic market. In light of this evidence, regulators should not deter foreign bidders, but rather welcome their entry.

III.1 Introduction

III.1.1 Objective and Motivation

Over the past two decades the international banking industry has been subject to an unprecedented level of restructuring activities.[124] The largest part of this con-

---

124 Cf. e.g. Beitel/Schiereck (2006), p. 7, Cybo-Ottone/Murgia (2000), p. 832, and Pilloff (1996), p. 294.

solidation process took the form of mergers and acquisitions. Driven especially by harmonization efforts under the Single Market Program, such as the Second Banking Directive of 1989 and, more recently, the introduction of the European Monetary Union (EMU), an unprecedented level of consolidation activity has been reshaping the European banking industry as well.[125]

The consolidation trend is expected to continue in coming years as the main drivers behind it push to remain in existence. First, the rapid technological progress in information technology that provides increasing synergy potential as well as pressures from a growing number of educated shareholders and globalization in general, push corporate strategies towards growing externally through M&A.[126] Second, there is still an implicit bank overhang in Europe, and in relation to population figures, there are still almost twice as many banks in the European Union as compared to the United States.[127] And third, the European banking sector persists to be the most fragmented industry on a pan-European level.[128] The reason behind the latter argument is simple: Until present the bulk of M&A activity in Europe's financial industry occurred within national borders.[129] It is believed that banks first wanted to consolidate their national positions before acquiring across borders.[130] Additionally, cross-border deals, until recently, were perceived as providing limited synergy potential[131] and, moreover, as requiring additional skills and resources to cope with increased complexity as compared to domestic acquisitions.[132] Finally, due to the pivotal role of the banking industry, protectionist actions by regulators and governments in combination with implicit and explicit rules against foreign acquirers have hindered cross-border M&A.[133] Some even view protectionist actions as having been one of two main obstacles for cross-border consolidation within Europe's banking industry.[134]

However, the situation has changed considerably in recent years. Due to profound national consolidation in most European markets, there is almost no potential left for further domestic acquisitions, particularly in smaller EU-15 countries. To grow externally, banks will therefore increasingly have to consider acquiring

---

125 Cf. Altunbas/Ibanez (2004), p. 7.
126 Cf. e.g. Bank for International Settlements (2001), Belaisch et al. (2001), Berger/Demsetz/Strahan (1999), and Smith/Walter (1998).
127 Cf. Altunbas/Ibanez (2004), p. 7.
128 Cf. Serra et al. (2005), p. 1.
129 Cf. Cabral/Dierick/Vesala (2002), p. 40.
130 Cf. European Central Bank (2000), p. 5.
131 Cf. Serra (2005), p. 6.
132 Cf. European Central Bank (2000), p. 6.
133 Cf. Berger/DeYoung/Udell (2001), p. 117, and Atkins (2005), w/p.
134 Cf. Serra (2005), p. 6.

foreign targets.[135] Moreover, cross-border acquisitions are perceived to finally have an increasingly beneficial economic rationale and, at the same time, domestic regulators of European countries are expected to have weakening possibilities to fend off foreign bidders.[136] As a result, cross-border M&A among banking institutions are expected to significantly increase in the European Union in the coming years.[137] The large cross-border acquisitions of UK Abbey National by Spanish Banco Santander in 2004 as well as of German Hypovereinsbank (HVB) by Italian Unicredit in 2005 are good examples of recently accelerating cross-border consolidation in Europe.

Despite the unprecedented level of consolidation in Europe's banking industry in the past two decades, only a few studies shed light on the wealth effects of European banking M&A.[138] Additionally, virtually all studies focus on bidder and targets and thereby ignore the effects M&A might have on the industry as a whole. There is no single capital market study which analyzes the effects of banking M&A on the entire European financial industry. There is also a lack of evidence concerning external effects of the accelerating cross-border M&A, which are still often viewed as threatening for the domestic banking industry by national governments and regulators alike. The present study wants to fill this research gap as it provides empirical arguments to the discussion and thereby attempts to clarify the negative prejudice on the effects of foreign entry. It is the first study that analyzes the full effects of M&A announcements not only on a domestic level but also gives an explicit assessment of their effects on a pan-European basis.

In the analysis the following questions are addressed: Do cross-border acquisitions between European banks create value for bidders and targets? Do these transactions also have effects on domestic and other European rival banks?

To assess the proposed research questions, an event study is conducted, one which analyzes share price reactions of both bidders and targets to announcements of cross-border M&A in Europe. The key addition of this study is, however, that it also assesses the reactions of a large portfolio of publicly listed European rival banks to the same announcements. The analysis is based on 51 cross-border M&A transactions that occurred between 1990 and 2005. This transaction sample is then broadened to a portfolio of up to 122 European rival banks for each announcement. Findings indicate that target shareholders enjoy a significant positive revaluation of their shares, whereas bidder returns are insignificant. Effects on rival banks are found to be positive and significant. Although being

---

135   Cf. European Central Bank (2004), p. 9.
136   Cf. Serra (2005), p. 6.
137   Cf. Serra et al. (2005), p. 1, and European Central Bank (2004), p. 9–10.
138   Cf. section III.3.1 for an overview.

strongest in the domestic market, a positive rival effect can also be observed across European borders.

III.1.2 Course of the Investigation

The course of the investigation is structured as follows: First, section III.2 lays out necessary background knowledge on the European banking market. Section III.2.1 illustrates the historic development of Europe's banking industry which led to a large degree of heterogeneity of national markets and also explains the various harmonization and deregulation efforts that have been undertaken under the Single Market Program (which have led to the present state of the industry). Section III.2.2 then provides a detailed overview of the unprecedented consolidation process during the last two decades within the European banking industry and provides an outlook of how and why the number of cross-border M&A is especially expected to grow in the future.

In the next step, a literature review on both applicable strands of research and the development of the hypotheses is provided in chapter III.3. Section III.3.1 presents prior research on banking M&A with a special focus on event studies covering the European market. Section III.3.2 then portrays prior research on rival effects by focusing on the three main hypotheses that have been discussed in the literature as the source for wealth effects at competing firms. Section III.3.3 then combines these two strands of research from the previous sections to develop the hypotheses that are tested in the event study.

The event study is then carried out in section III.4. Chosen event study methodology is described in section III.4.1, before sample and data selection criteria as well as rival portfolio composition are laid out in section III.4.2. Descriptive statistics of the analyzed transaction sample are provided in section III.4.3. Finally, results of the event study for both targets and bidders as well as those for the rival portfolio and rival subsamples are presented in section III.4.4, which are then discussed and interpreted in section III.4.5.

Section III.5 wraps up the findings and concludes the essay.

III.2 The European Banking Market

III.2.1 Heterogeneity, Harmonization, and Deregulation

Due to diverse developments of the late 19th century within today's EU membership countries, the European Banking market had historically grown to be quite heterogeneous.[139] At that time, the bi-polar system of town-based banks focusing on trade financing and country-based banks focusing instead on local, mostly agricultural financing was brought about to change by means of the industrial revolution. The industrialization led to an increasing importance of town-based banks and the development of financial centers, such as London or Frankfurt, as well as to the creation of nationwide branch structures, which were owned by town-based banks.

As a result, competition grew between regional country-based banks on one side and national town-based banks on the other, which of course took different forms in the individual countries and thereby led to heterogeneous developments in European banking. These developments also led to a variety of individual regulatory and accounting systems amongst the different European countries.[140] In addition, the relationship between banks and industry were the opposite in the UK compared to continental Europe. Whereas in continental Europe banks put their main focus on industry financing, UK banks rather focused on trade financing, which left UK's industry in need to turn to the capital markets for funding (similar to the US). For this reason continental Europe's economy is usually referred to as a bank-based system as opposed to the market-based system in the UK.[141] An important additional element of heterogeneity was the existence of individual currencies in most European countries, which separated money markets in terms of rates and currency.[142] As a consequence of the above factors, the European Banking market had grown to be quite heterogeneous along many dimensions.

Since as early as 1957, when the Treaty of Rome was signed, an increasing number of European countries have been aiming to establish a common market within Europe.[143] Because of its central role, the integration of the financial industry has always been at the core of this development. Numerous legal changes that started in the 1970s were introduced to harmonize the diverse regulatory and supervisory systems. This sequence of changes, which made it easier and – most importantly – cheaper for banks to operate across European borders, is usually referred to as the Single Market Program (SMP). However, the First Banking Directive of 1977 (the 1985 White Paper as well as the 1986 Single European Act) achieved little in terms of harmonizing national regulatory systems.

---

139 For this and the following cf. Sander/Kleimeier (2001), p. 2–4, if not stated otherwise.
140 Cf. European Central Bank (2000), p. 6.
141 Cf. Bikker/Wesseling (2003), p. 4.
142 Cf. Gardener/Molyneux/Moore (1998), p. 94.
143 For this and the next paragraph cf. Sander/Kleimeier (2001), p. 3–4, and Berger/DeYoung/Udell (2001), p. 118–119, if not stated otherwise.

It was not until the Second Banking Directive (SBD) of 1989 was implemented that harmonization and deregulation[144] successes were first being achieved. The SBD put its focus on harmonization, mutual recognition and home country control. In particular, harmonization implied that banks operating in more than one European country would be subject to a common set of EU regulations. Secondly, mutual recognition effectively introduced a single EU banking license by allowing national banking charters to be sufficient for operations throughout the entire EU. And thirdly, home country rule implied that banks operating in more than one European country were solely regulated by their home country. As a result, after the implementation of the SBD in 1993/1994, universal banking became the European standard; any nation that did not comply would put its domestic banks at a comparative disadvantage.

Additional directives were introduced in the following years to further support harmonization and deregulation efforts by enabling the development of a single securities market as well as the establishment of a "single passport for investment firms".[145] However, the arguably most important measure towards integrating European markets and creating a single market taken in the last decade was the creation of the European Monetary Union (EMU). Introducing a single currency for most markets also enabled a single monetary policy and thereby a common basic interest rate controlled by only one central bank – the European Central Bank (ECB). The former more than a dozen individual national financial markets – each with its own currency – were being integrated through the creation of the Euro to create a combined financial market for twelve of the then 15 member states.[146] It was now possible to borrow and lend in different parts of the EU at the same money market rate without the necessity of currency conversion.[147] Concurrent with this argument, Perez, Salas-Fumar, and Saurina (2005) find evidence that the creation of the Euro has increased integration speed of the European banking industry.[148]

---

144 Evidence suggests that increasing intra- and interstate deregulation increases the number of potential bidders, which improves the market for corporate control and thereby leads to greater market discipline of banks, reduced market share for poor performing banks and raises profitability, on average. Cf. e.g. Hubbard/Palia (1995), Jayaratne/Strahan (1998), and Schranz (1993). Concurrent with this argument, European banking M&A predominantly occurred between large, profitable banks acquiring smaller banks with poor efficiency levels. Cf. e.g. Beitel/Schiereck/Wahrenburg (2004), Focarelli/Panetta/Salleo (2002), and Vander Vennet (1997).

145 Berger/DeYoung/Udell (2001), p. 118.

146 Cf. Perez/Salas-Fumas/Saurina (2005), p. 9.

147 Cf. Gardener/Molyneux/Moore (1998), p. 94.

148 Cf. Perez/Salas-Fumas/Saurina (2005), p. 8–28.

Another step taken to harmonize European regulation standards was the agreement for a single takeover code, which was reached in November 2003 after negotiations had been dragging on for 14 (!) years.[149] However, this measure did not yield the desired result, as it left the adoption of key items of the takeover code optional for EU member countries and thereby still provides flexibility for individual countries to take protectionist actions against foreign bidders.[150] This is particularly problematic as consolidation through M&A is a key element of Europe-wide integration of the banking industry. Cross-border consolidation is important for the individual national banking markets to grow together across borders and thereby foster the creation of a single market for financial services within Europe. The next chapter will therefore focus on consolidation in the European banking industry that accompanied the harmonization and deregulation efforts of the past decades (which are outlined in this chapter).

To conclude, the historically grown heterogeneity of the European banking market has tried to progress by attempting the creation of a single European market. The numerous harmonization and deregulation efforts taken within the SMP had limited success in the beginning, but started to show first achievements with the implementation of the SBD. The creation of the EMU along with the introduction of a common European currency increased the speed of integration and could soon lead to a much more integrated financial industry on a pan-European basis.

III.2.2 Consolidation and Cross-Border M&A

The competitive forces brought upon the European Banking industry through the introduction of the SMP, amongst other things, were driving European banks towards consolidation.[151] As the SMP changed the cost economies that EU banks could reap through economies of scale as well as other benefits of size[152], mergers and acquisitions became an attractive strategy to benefit from this development. At the same time, the accelerating integration of the European financial industry as well as deregulation put competitive pressure on the banks to become more efficient and profitable. The integration thereby enforced the strategic trend towards M&A. Further drivers that have been identified as fostering consolidation are the rapid technological progress in information technology (IT), the

---

149 This demonstrates how difficult it can be to reach harmonization agreements amongst a large group of European countries which might have differing objectives.
150 Cf. Campa/Hernando (2004), p. 49.
151 Cf. Altunbas/Ibanez (2004), p. 7.
152 Cf. Altunbas/Molyneux (1996), p. 217–218.

growing education of and pressure from shareholders, improvements in financial condition of banks, the introduction of the EMU, international consolidation of markets as well as globalization in general.[153]

As a result of the developments mentioned above, the European banking industry has witnessed a sharp increase in M&A-transactions and the European banking market has been subject to an increasing level of consolidation.[154] Within this restructuring phase of the banking industry, the number of credit institutions decreased significantly. For example, in the period from 1997 to 2003, their number reduced by 2,200 institutions to a little less than 7,500 at the end of 2003. Most of this 23% decrease is attributable to M&As. At the same time, the size of an average credit institution almost doubled to a level of €3.5 billion of assets. Although the years 1998 to 2000 – driven by the introduction of the EMU as well as the boom at the capital markets – had been the strongest in terms of the number of M&A deals as well as average transaction volume, M&A activity again stabilized in 2003 after the capital market crashes in 2001 and 2002. The consolidation trend is unbroken, but recently appears to be changing in its nature.

Until present, the bulk of M&A activity in the European banking sector occurred within national borders.[155] For example, between 1990 and 2001, 78% of the aggregate M&A transaction value was accounted for by domestic deals.[156] There are several arguments why consolidation primarily occurred within national borders until present: First, banks may have wanted to initially consolidate their national market positions before making the strategic move across borders.[157] Second, domestic deals are believed to deliver superior synergy potential through possible restructuring of overlapping branch structures and customer migration. At the same time, cost cutting potential is assumed to be limited in cross-border transactions.[158] Moreover, when acquiring foreign targets, bidders have to cope with differences in culture, language, currency (before the EMU), as well as existing differences in regulatory and accounting systems. This adds complexity and costs to an M&A transaction and requires better skills as well as significant

---

153 Cf. e.g. Bank for International Settlements (2001), Belaisch et al. (2001), Berger/ Demsetz/Strahan (1999) and Smith/Walter (1998).
154 For this paragraph cf. European Central Bank (2004), p. 8.
155 Cf. e.g. Berger/DeYoung/Udell (2001), p.117–118, European Central Bank (2000), p. 5, and Serra (2005), p. 5.
156 Cf. Cabral/Dierick/Vesala (2002), p. 40.
157 Cf. European Central Bank (2000), p. 5.
158 Cf. Serra (2005), p. 6.

resources compared to domestic deals.[159] Finally, the legal situation is more complex as takeover codes still differ among EU member states.[160]

Another line of argument points towards the political dimension of cross-border deals. As banking is perceived as a strategic industry having a pivotal role by providing financing to the industrial companies of each country,[161] domestic regulators had the vision of creating national banking champions that can also succeed on a European level.[162] Viewing foreign competition as destabilizing the domestic market, foreign bidders were tried to be blocked.[163] This was achieved through explicit or implicit regulations[164] as well as protective actions of both regulators and politicians.[165] Morgan Stanley even believes that nationalistic arguments brought forward by domestic regulators (and politicians) against foreign bidders have been one of the two main obstacles for cross-border consolidation in Europe.[166] The other main obstacle is assumed to be the lack of a clear economic rationale for the value creation through cross-border acquisitions.

However, in the same report it is argued that both of these obstacles are increasingly disappearing.[167] First, the EU Competition and Internal Market commissioners have stressed that the EU banking directive, which has the creation of a free and integrated European banking market at its core, must not face any obstacles in theory and practice. Domestic regulators should therefore from now on have greater difficulties in giving the necessary weight to their nationalistic arguments. Secondly, Morgan Stanley believes that cross-border acquisitions finally do have a beneficial economic rationale, which is required to get shareholder approval for the envisaged acquisition. In particular, synergy potential through IT integration as well as diversification advantages arising through Basel II are expected to provide sufficient benefits. As a consequence, Morgan Stanley expects to see more cross-border consolidation starting in 2005/2006. The European Central Bank has a similar view, but takes a different approach.[168] In its view, banks will have to turn their focus towards cross-border M&A simply be-

---

159   Cf. European Central Bank (2000), p. 6.
160   Cf. Campa/Hernando (2004), p. 48.
161   Cf. Altunbas/Ibanez (2004), p. 5.
162   Cf. Williams/Thurm (2004), p. 33–34. To foster the creation of national banking champions, regulators and governments also promoted national consolidation and thereby not only hindered cross-border M&A, but also pushed towards domestic consolidation.
163   Cf. Serra (2005), p. 6.
164   Cf. Berger/DeYoung/Udell (2001), p. 117.
165   Cf. Atkins (2005), w/p.
166   Cf. Serra (2005), p. 6.
167   Cf. Serra (2005), p. 6.
168   Cf. European Central Bank (2004), p. 9–10.

cause domestic markets have already become quite concentrated. Particularly the smaller member countries are perceived to have almost no potential left for any further domestic concentration.[169] There are only a few countries left, such as Germany and Italy, which are believed to still have potential for domestic consolidation.[170]

To conclude, the European banking industry has been subject to significant consolidation activity since the beginning of the 1990s. Until recently the large majority of M&A transactions occurred within national borders as banks seem to have focused on consolidating domestic positions before turning to cross-border acquisitions. In addition, the interference of regulators aiming at creating national banking champions as well as the lack of an apparent economic rationale have mostly prohibited the occurrence of non-domestic transactions. However, as most national markets have limited or no potential left for further concentration and as main obstacles for cross-border consolidation are disappearing, there is broad consensus that the consolidation trend is increasingly pointing across borders within Europe's banking industry. The large cross-border acquisitions of UK Abbey National by Spanish Banco Santander in 2004 as well as that of German HVB by Italian Unicredit in 2005, which was also viewed positively in the market,[171] are good examples of accelerating cross-border consolidation in Europe. Indeed, it can be said that "European banks look ripe for [cross-border] consolidation."[172]

III.3 Literature Review and Hypotheses Generation

This chapter first provides a literature review covering the large amount of research that has been conducted on M&A in the banking industry. After a general introduction on the reasoning behind M&A, US and especially European event studies are presented. Second, as this is the main focus of this study, prior research on external effects that M&A can have on rival companies are discussed in detail. Finally, these two strands of research are combined to lead to the formulation of specific hypotheses regarding rival effects of cross-border M&A in the European banking industry, which are tested in the event study.

---

169 For concentration indicators of national banking markets cf. European Central Bank (2000), p. 18.
170 Cf. Serra (2005), p. 5.
171 Cf. Serra/Zadra (2005), p. 1–4.
172 Cf. Serra et al. (2005), p. 1.

III.3.1 M&A in the Banking Industry

It is common knowledge that the banking industry has been going through a phase of profound restructuring in the past two decades.[173] Most of the restructuring activities took the form of M&A. This consolidation trend started in the US and subsequently made its way to Europe in the 1990s. As mentioned before, the consolidation trend in Europe continues to hold steadily and is expected to do so in the coming years. The motive bidder management provides for an envisaged acquisition usually refers to synergies and value maximization that ultimately would result in wealth increases for shareholders of the involved entities. The consolidated entity is then believed to be worth more than the two individual banks if kept separate. The two main reasons behind this rationale are supposed to be improvement of performance and reduction of risk.[174] Risk should be reduced through the combination of earnings having a lower volatility than individually. Performance improvements can generally be achieved in various ways: First, in an efficient market for corporate control, acquiring banks having higher quality management will lead the target bank to improved performance levels. Second, performance can improve through the elimination of redundancies in the organization, which raises efficiency levels by now being able to offer an advanced product and service mix. This argument therefore refers to the exploitation of economies of scale and scope. Finally, performance can improve through an acquisition resulting in an increase in the market and thereby in pricing power.

However, merging two different, formerly independent entities can prove to be a difficult exercise. Differences e.g. in culture, processes and procedures might pose significant challenges. In addition, a consolidation trend might also reinforce its own development. Managers could simply feel obliged to engage an acquisition in order to keep pace with industry consolidation or to avoid becoming a target themselves.[175] This leads to the second type of motive for consolidation activities besides value maximization: The opposite group of non-value maximizing motives, particularly those that managers might be able and willing to pursue for own their private objectives when deciding for or against an acquisition. As their compensation (as well as their perceived status) tends to rise with increasing firm size, they might engage an acquisition strategy for their own private benefit.[176] This acquisition motive is usually referred to as empire building.

---

173 Cf. e.g. Beitel/Schiereck (2006), p. 7, and Cybo-Ottone/Murgia (2000), p. 832.
174 For the remainder of this argument cf. Pilloff (1996), p. 294–295.
175 Cf. Pilloff (1996), p. 295.
176 Cf. Berger/Demsetz/Strahan (1999), p. 146.

In addition, managers could be subject to hubris as they might overestimate their skills regarding, particularly the integration of the target, and thereby the potential for synergies.[177] On the other hand, target managers could also try to block otherwise value maximizing acquisitions in order to secure their positions. Hadlock, Houston, and Ryngaert (1999) find that banks in which executives hold a greater share of the equity are less likely to become a target.[178] This motive is usually referred to as management entrenchment. In addition to some other non-value maximizing motives that originate from the managers, such as the Free Cash Flow Hypothesis proposed by Jensen,[179] governments can also exert their influence. As discussed in the previous chapter, government or regulator intervention was perceived as one of the main obstacles for cross-border consolidation in Europe's banking industry.

As a result, the motives behind observed M&A can be manifold and do not necessarily need to be oriented at value maximization. Non-value maximizing motives of managers and others, such as the government, can also play an important role and evidence suggests they do. Albeit results are being widely dispersed, M&A seem to not create or even destroy shareholder value for the acquiring bank.[180] Positive wealth effects in the aggregate (if any) mostly accrue to the target company. Considering the large number of M&A transactions that occurred in the last almost three decades, as described above, these empirical results lead to a paradox: Although M&A transactions seem not to create (or even destroy) value for the shareholders of the bidder, a large number of banks continue to engage in acquisition strategies. Literature provides numerous possible explanations to resolve this puzzle.[181] However, due to so many studies applying various methodologies, which all come to similar results, the influence of non-value maximizing motives on banking M&A can not be negated.

Prior research on the success of banking M&A will be outlined in detail in the following. There are generally three different approaches on how to assess the success of an M&A transactions: Capital market oriented event study, performance study and dynamic efficiency study.[182] As only the event study approach is able to directly calculate the impact of M&A on shareholder value and as it is

---

177   The hubris theory was introduced by Roll (1986), p. 197–216.
178   Cf. Hadlock/Houston/Ryngaert (1999), p. 221–249.
179   Cf. Jensen (1986), p. 323–329.
180   For an overview cf. e.g. Pilloff/Santomero (1998), Beitel (2002), and Beitel/Schiereck (2003).
181   Most of these explanations relate to methodological failures and data biases. Cf. e.g. Calomiris (1999), Calomiris/Karceski (1998), and Pilloff/Santomero (1998).
182   For an overview of the three different approaches cf. Beitel/Schiereck (2003), p. 502–506.

therefore the approach chosen for this paper, the following discussion mainly focuses on results of prior event studies on M&A in the banking industry.

Until present, most studies on banking M&A have focused on the US market; the European evidence is still rather limited. Pilloff and Santomero (1998) as well as Beitel and Schiereck (2003) provide a comprehensive overview of the large number of empirical studies covering the US market.[183] Overall, results are quite varied. Nevertheless, most studies point towards negative or insignificant wealth effects for the bidders and clearly positive wealth effects for the targets. Houston and Ryngaert (1994) find small negative effects for the bidders and positive effects for the targets.[184] However, combined weighted average gains to both bidders and targets are insignificant. Another study finds contradictory evidence for M&As, in which banks of similar geographic area and activity scope merge.[185] In this type of transaction, significant value is created for the combined entity at announcement.

The still limited research on M&A in European banking has been growing considerably in recent years as a number of empirical studies have been published. To the best of the author's knowledge, there are currently nine event studies covering the European market. In the first study, Tourani-Rad and van Beek (1999) analyze European bank M&A transactions between 1989 and 1996 and find that target bank shareholders experience significant positive abnormal returns whereas bidders experience insignificant returns.[186] Furthermore, returns for bidders become increasingly positive with growing size and efficiency of the acquirer. Findings also indicate that effects of cross-border acquisitions are not significantly different from those of domestic transactions.

In another study, Cybo-Ottone and Murgia (2000) analyze a sample of 54 M&A transactions that took place in 14 European banking markets from 1988 to 1997.[187] They calculate abnormal returns for the combined entity of bidder and target and find a positive wealth effect that is statistically significant, indicating that transactions in their sample were overall successful.

Beitel and Schiereck (2006) analyze the value implications of 98 M&A transactions which occurred between 1985 and 2000 in the European banking industry.[188] Results are similar as they also indicate a wealth increase for the combined entity. Consistent with US research, they additionally find a considerable and sig-

183   Cf. Pilloff/Santomero (1998) and Beitel/Schiereck (2003) for an overview.
184   Cf. Houston/Ryngaert (1994), p. 1155–1176.
185   Cf. DeLong (2001), p. 221–252.
186   Cf. Tourani-Rad/van Beek (1999), p. 532–540.
187   Cf. Cybo-Ottone/Murgia (2000), p. 831–859.
188   Cf. Beitel/Schiereck (2006), p. 7–29. This study had previously been published as a working paper in 2001 and is therefore included at this point of the review.

nificant positive wealth effect for target shareholders. On the other hand, effects for bidders were insignificantly different from zero. Moreover, their results indicate that large deals that occurred since 1998 accumulated significant negative returns. Even more, they find European cross-border acquisitions to be value destroying. A further analysis of the same data sample in Beitel, Schiereck, and Wahrenburg (2004) yields evidence showing that focused transactions lead to more positive returns, and that frequent bidders experience significantly smaller returns.[189] This indicates that managers of frequent bidding banks are possibly being motivated by non-value maximizing motives.

Lepetit, Patry, and Rous (2004) examine a total of 180 M&A transactions that occurred from 1991 to 2001 in 13 European banking markets.[190] They document that targets exhibit a positive and significant revaluation of their shares. Moreover, transactions with cross-product diversification or geographic specialization lead to positive market reactions, whereas focusing transactions and those leading to geographic diversification result in no significant market reaction. This is somewhat contradictory evidence when compared to the results found by Beitel, Schiereck, and Wahrenburg (2004), as in their study, focusing transactions lead to superior wealth effects.[191]

Beitel, Lorenz, and Schiereck (2005) conduct an event study on a sample of 71 European M&A transactions in the banking industry covering the period from 1990 to 2002.[192] Results indicate that bidders, on average, were five times larger than targets. Wealth effects were found to be clearly positive for targets, small negative for bidders and in the aggregate, slightly positive for the combined entity. Interestingly, they also provide evidence that cross-border transactions within the EU were value destroying.

In contrast to the above studies, Ismail and Davidson (2005) find weak evidence that there are higher positive wealth effects for cross-border deals than for domestic ones, indicating benefits from geographic diversification.[193] They analyze a total of 102 M&A announcements of transactions that took place from 1987 to 1999. On average, returns to targets are again found to be positive, but smaller when compared to other studies. Wealth effects for bidders vary widely depending on the type of deal and on average are slightly positive.

Caruso and Palmucci (2005) study a rather small sample of 21 domestic M&A transactions that occurred within the Italian market in the period from

---

189   Cf. Beitel/Schiereck/Wahrenburg (2004), p. 109–139.
190   Cf. Lepetit/Patry/Rous (2004), p. 663–669.
191   Cf. Beitel/Schiereck/Wahrenburg (2004), p. 109–139.
192   Cf. Beitel/Lorenz/Schiereck (2005).
193   Cf. Ismail/Davidson (2005), p. 13–30.

1994 to 2003.[194] In the aggregate, they do not find evidence indicating a significant value creation for the combined entity. As seen in other studies, returns to target shareholders are positive and returns to bidder shareholders negative. Again, value seems to have been redistributed from bidder to target shareholders. The authors interpret this as an indication of bidder banks' management, amongst other things, looking for empire building.

Finally, Campa and Hernando (2006) analyze a large sample of European banking M&A that took place from 1998 to 2002.[195] Results again indicate that target shareholders enjoy positive wealth effects at announcement whereas bidder shareholders, on average, exhibit slightly negative returns. Within their analysis the authors also document that target banks significantly improve both return on equity and operational efficiency after being acquired. Since before the transaction, targets, on average, exhibit lower performance levels as compared to the sector average and the bidding banks in particular, there seems to be an efficient market for corporate control in the banking industry. As envisaged by the Single Market Program and the EMU, consolidation seems to improve performance levels of the targets and thereby the banking industry as a whole.

Table III.1 provides an overview of the prior research studies that have been presented above.

To conclude, prior research on banking M&A still is somewhat limited for the European market. However, a growing number of studies are being published and the nine existing studies already allow some general conclusions to be drawn. Overall, it seems that M&A transactions in the European banking industry create little or no value for the combined entity and sometimes are even values destroying. Target shareholders can generally enjoy small to significantly positive wealth effects, whereas those for bidder shareholders are either close to zero or negative. Evidence concerning the type of acquisition is still contradictory. No clear picture can be drawn concerning the expectations of wealth effects from focusing versus diversifying M&A. Although most studies point towards negative returns for the combined entity of cross-border M&A, one study found positive returns. As former obstacles for cross-border M&A of the 1990s are increasingly disappearing, these transactions could be more often value creating in the future. The effects on rivals and thereby the industry as a whole is a different story than the effects on directly involved parties. Rival effects of cross-border M&A could already have been positive in the consolidation of the European banking market from the early 1990s until present. The following section therefore outlines potential effects of M&A announcements on rival companies and thereby leads to-

---

194 Cf. Caruso/Palmucci (2005).
195 Cf. Campa/Hernando (2006), p. 3367–3392.

wards the formulation of the hypotheses being developed in the last section of this chapter.

Table III.1: Prior Event Study Research on European Banking M&A

Paper	Time Period	Summary of Results
Tourani-Rad/van Beek (1999)	1989–1996	Bidders experience insignificant wealth effects and targets enjoy significant positive wealth effects.
Cybo-Ottone/Murgia (2000)	1988–1997	Significant positive wealth effects for the combined entity.
Beitel/Schiereck (2006)	1985–2000	Bidders experience insignificant wealth effects and targets enjoy significant positive wealth effects. Wealth increase for the combined entity. Cross-boarder acquisitions are value destroying.
Beitel/Schiereck/Wahrenburg (2004)	1985–2000	Focussed transactions lead to more positive returns. Frequent bidders experience smaller returns.
Beitel/Lorenz/Schiereck (2000?)	1990–2002	Bidders experience small and insignificant negative wealth effects and targets enjoy large significant wealth effects. On aggregate marginal positive value is created for the combined entity.
Lepetit/Patry/Rous (2004)	1991–2001	Bidders experience insignificant wealth effects and targets enjoy significant positive wealth effects. Focussed and geographic diversification transactions do not lead to positive effects, but diversifying and geographically specializing M&A do.
Ismail/Davidson (2005)	1987–1999	Bidders experience slightly positive wealth effects and targets enjoy significant, but in relation to other studies comparably smaller wealth effects. Weak evidence for positive effects of cross-boarder M&A.
Caruso/Palmucci (2005)	1994–2003	Bidders experience negative wealth effects and targets enjoy positive wealth effects. No significant value creation for the combined entity.
Campa/Hernando (2006)	1998–2002	Bidders experience slightly negative wealth effects and targets enjoy positive wealth effects. Target banks improve ROE and operational efficiency after being acquired.

Source: Personal summary in the style of Zietz/Sirmans/Friday (2003), p. 129–134.

III.3.2 Effects of M&A Announcements on Rivals

The action of one company (or more companies) generally does not only affect itself; actions of greater importance, such as M&A, can usually have an effect on the industry as a whole as it e.g. might change competitive conditions. Thereby, it can convey information signals to the market that rivals in the same industry are also affected by this very action. Only if these external effects of an M&A announcement are included in the analysis can the total effect of consolidation on an industry be measured.[196] Pioneered by Eckbo (1983) and Stillman (1983), a large body of literature has analyzed share price reactions of competing firms to M&A announcements within their industry.[197] Interestingly enough, virtually all studies found that rivals experience positive wealth effects when a competitor is being acquired, which implies that the industry as a whole benefits from M&A.

The remainder of this chapter provides an overview of the main hypothesis that prior research has tested to explain the observed abnormal rival returns. They can be subsumed under the following three headings: Market power, efficiency, and acquisition probability.

Market Power

Although it is often difficult to identify the ultimate goals of M&A participants, there is evidence that some acquisition strategies aim at increasing market power.[198] Vigorous enforcement of antitrust laws, both in the US and the European Union, aims to prevent increases of market power, which is believed to generally come at the expense of the customers. Antitrust policy was and still is based on the market concentration doctrine,[199] which is an implication of the first economic oligopoly models put forward by Cournot (1838) and Nash (1950).[200] Within this school of thought, market power is expected to increase as horizontal mergers allow the merging firms (and the rivals) to increase their own wealth at the expense of customers and suppliers. Stigler (1964) was the first to explicitly point out that in an oligopoly, the number of independent companies within an industry is inversely related to the ability to enforce pre-determined price agreements.[201] For example, with a decrease of independent competitors (increase in concentration), effective collusion among market participants becomes more eas-

---

196 Cf. Berger/Demsetz/Strahan (1999), p. 137.
197 Cf. e.g. Eckbo (1983, 1985, and 1992), Song/Walkling (2000), and Stillman (1983).
198 Cf. Berger/Demsetz/Strahan (1999), p. 144.
199 Cf. Eckbo (1985), p. 325.
200 Cf. Cournot (1838) and Nash (1950).
201 For this and the following cf. Stigler (1964), p. 44–46.

ily achievable. Relatively high levels of industry concentration, in combination with the presence of entry barriers, can thereby lead to dominant firm pricing on both in- and output level,[202] which would be associated with skimming of industry-wide monopoly rents. Increased profitability of the participants then leads to the adherence to such collusion agreements and provides short-run stability to the emerged cartel.

Eckbo (1983) and Stillman (1983) were the first to apply this theory to shareholder wealth effects on rivals of horizontally merging peers in their pioneering studies.[203] Within their frameworks, horizontal mergers should result in a positive wealth effect for the rivals, as they are expected to benefit from increased industry concentration levels as these increase market power and the probability of effective collusion. This wealth effect is expected, regardless of whether a firm takes or does not take part in the collusion agreement, as in the latter case it would simply free-ride on higher product prices. Interestingly, despite being the most cited hypothesis for positive rival effects, all capital market studies reject the collusion hypothesis, leaving the explanation for these effects unclear.[204] In addition, these studies fail to explain the large cross-section variation in abnormal rival returns as well as the fact that only 50–60% of rivals exhibited positive wealth effects.[205] This led to the search of other possible explanations for positive rival effects, which will be explained below. However, studies focusing on other measures than stock prices, such as ticket fares in the airline industry or deposit rates in the banking industry, find evidence that indicates market power increases arising from horizontal mergers.[206]

Efficiency

In contrast to the above statements, an M&A transaction could also have negative wealth effects on rival companies. If an acquisition leads to increased efficiency and profitability levels of the larger combined entity, increased competition should ultimately result in lower product and higher factor prices. As the literature review on banking M&A showed, it is common that targets have below aver-

---

202   On the input level, some authors have analyzed the possible effects of increased pricing power that can be exerted on suppliers. However, since being less prevalent in research and also not being truly applicable for the banking industry, the discussion in this section refrains from this part of the market power hypothesis. For detailed discussion cf. e.g. Fee/Thomas (2004) and Sharur (2003).
203   Cf. Eckbo (1983), p. 241–273, and Stillman (1983), p. 225–240.
204   Cf. e.g. Eckbo (1983, 1985, 1992), Fee/Thomas (2004), and Stillman (1983).
205   Cf. Song/Walkling (2000), p. 144.
206   Cf. e.g. Singal (1996) and Prager/Hannan (1998).

age performance levels which improve after the merger. Efficiency enhancements should then lead to a more competitive environment within the industry in which it becomes more difficult for competitors, at least in the short run, to maintain their level of performance.[207] As a result, a M&A transaction could lead to competitors losing market shares and thereby result in negative abnormal returns for the rival firms at announcement.[208]

However, the relationship within the efficiency hypothesis is not one-sided. As, by definition, competitors have similar production technologies as well as operational procedures, an M&A announcement can also provide an information signal to the market that rival firms have potential to similarly increase their own efficiency.[209] Concurrent with this argument, Claessens, Demirgüc-Kunt, and Huizinga (2001) show that (in most countries), when a foreign bank acquires a domestic bank, the remaining domestic banks exhibit an increase in profitability levels.[210] Rivals can thereby benefit from efficiency spill-over effects from the more efficient peer company. As a result, a positive wealth effect is similarly possible under the efficiency hypothesis.[211]

A central problem cited by Eckbo (1983) is that the market power and the efficiency hypotheses are not mutually exclusive.[212] Any observed rival returns can be viewed as the sum of effects under both hypotheses. However, as rival returns were found to be similarly positive for vertical and horizontal mergers, the author concluded that the observed gains were the result of anticipated future cost-savings and not increased market power. Eckbo (1983) thereby implicitly states that anticipated future efficiency gains outweigh the possible negative rival effect of increased competition. As a result, under the efficiency hypothesis, positive returns for rival companies can also be expected.

Acquisition Probability

As both market power and efficiency hypothesis fail to fully explain the empirical evidence presented above, Eckbo (1992) was the first to point towards another possible explanation. Because he had difficulties to assert the positive rival returns of 89 non-horizontal Canadian mergers, he suggested that an M&A announcement might provide a signal that an industry-specific resource had become more valuable, which would therefore increase the acquisition probability of

---

207   Cf. Campa/Hernando (2005), p. 11.
208   Cf. Bohl/Havrylchyk/Schiereck (2006), p. 81.
209   Cf. Eckbo (1983), p. 244.
210   Cf. Claessens/Demirgüc-Kunt/Huizinga (2001), p. 891.
211   Cf. Eckbo (1983), p. 244.
212   For this and the following cf. Eckbo (1983), p. 245–269.

competitors of the target.[213] Song/Walking (2000) tested the acquisition probability hypothesis in their study.[214] In their framework, an M&A announcement provides a signal to the market that there is a value differential for at least one firm in the industry.[215] Since the bidder is willing to pay a premium for the target regardless whether this differential relates to synergy potential or bad target management, the acquisition causes an industry shock, which results in a probability assessment for potential acquisitions of rival companies. Implications are different (in contrast to the market power hypothesis), as positive rival returns occur irrespectively of whether the transaction was horizontal or successful.

Empirical evidence provided by Song/Walking (2000) supports the acquisition probability hypothesis.[216] Rivals indeed exhibit positive wealth effects regardless of the form and success of the acquisition. Interestingly, rival returns increase both with the magnitude of surprise of the acquisition as well as for rivals which later on become targets themselves. As suggested in their framework, the market seems to judge the acquisition probability for each rival individually. In a broader study, Akhigbe/Madura (1999) find positive wealth effects for competitors, which were significantly related to firm- and industry-specific characteristics that reflect the individual probability of being acquired.[217]

Virtually all studies that have analyzed the effects of M&A announcements on rival firms found, on average, positive shareholder returns. Only two event studies, amongst other things, analyzed rival effects in the banking industry. In their analysis of foreign acquisitions of Polish banks, Bohl/Havrylchyk/Schiereck (2006) find positive returns for domestic rivals, which the authors mainly attribute to an increase in acquisition probability.[218] Campa/Hernando (2005) find contradictory evidence, as in their study, abnormal returns are found to be close to zero in the short-term and become positive in the long-run. [219] However, due to the wide dispersion of results, returns are insignificant. As these findings clearly stand out from the rest of the rival effects literature and as their study is still in a preliminary state using rather simple methodology, its findings are neglected in this study. The author therefore follows the reasoning of all other prior research on rival effects.

As outlined above, research has generally tested three different hypotheses to explain the observed positive shareholder wealth effects at rival companies. Ho-

213   Cf. Eckbo (1992), p. 1017.
214   Cf. Song/Walkling (2000), p. 143–171.
215   For this and the following cf. Song/Walkling (2000), p. 144.
216   Cf. Song/Walkling (2000), p. 143.
217   Cf. Akhigbe/Madura (1999), p. 1.
218   Cf. Bohl/Havrylchyk/Schiereck (2006), p. 80–85.
219   Cf. Campa/Hernando (2005), p. 1–20.

wever, particularly the market power hypothesis, which was tested the most, could not be validated with capital market data. Nevertheless, other studies focusing on product price data (as well as the fact that antitrust policy exists and is strictly enforced) point toward some stickiness of that hypothesis.[220] On the other hand, stronger evidence is found that is , particularly in favor of the acquisition probability as well as the efficiency hypothesis. The latter seems to be particularly applicable for the banking industry, as Claessens, Demirgüc-Kunt, and Huizinga (2001) show that foreign entry leads to efficiency increases at the rival banks as well.[221] Finally, it can be said that consolidation seems to lead towards higher levels of efficiency, raised valuation levels, and arguably more market power. Taking careful consideration of the latter, which is disapproved by most studies, the banking industry seems to benefit as a whole from consolidation. Consolidation resembling an efficient market for corporate control as well as an overall increased level of competition ultimately seems to result in a more robust banking industry.

III.3.3 Hypotheses Generation

As long as bank managers are acting in the best interest of their shareholders, both target and bidder shareholders should get additional value from an M&A transaction, as management would undertake it only under these conditions. Under the assumption that capital market participants can realistically gauge the influence of the transaction at announcement, the abnormal value increase should resemble both synergy potential and takeover premium as well as negotiation skills of both sides. However, as mentioned before, specific research on the banking industry provides a different view. Most studies for both the US as well as the European banking industry find no or rather small negative abnormal returns for the group of bidders.[222] It seems that other non-value maximizing motives also play a role in making corporate strategy decisions at banking institutions. The majority of related research additionally finds more profound negative bidder returns in cross-border acquisitions. As a result, within this analysis of cross-border M&A, concurrent with most previous literature, bidder returns are expected to be negative.

---

220   Cf. e.g. Singal (1996) and Prager/Hannan (1998).
221   Cf. Claessens/Demirgüc-Kunt/Huizinga (2001), p. 891–911.
222   As outlined in section III.3.1.

Hypothesis 1a)   The announcement has an abnormal negative effect on bidder share price.

Concerning the wealth effects for target bank shareholders, evidence of prior research is clearer cut. Overall, results indicate that targets enjoy significant positive abnormal returns. This should also still hold for cross-border M&A, because similar to domestic deals, the aim is to gain control of the target. As a result, the bidder will still have to pay a similar price as if he were a domestic acquirer in order to convince target shareholders. Additional costs incurred through increased complexity should instead decrease synergy potential and thereby destroy value only for the bidder. Taking defensive actions of regulators and/or governments into account, a cross-border acquirer could even be forced to pay a higher price in order to convince existing shareholders to tender. Accordingly, targets are expected to exhibit significantly positive returns at announcement.

Hypothesis 1b)   The announcement has an abnormal positive effect on target share price.

As mentioned before, an M&A transaction between two banks usually has an effect on competing firms and thereby on the industry as a whole. Including these external effects in the analysis allows the measurement of the total impact of the transaction. The literature review in section III.3.2. has shown that virtually all prior studies which have analyzed the effects of M&A announcements on competing firms found positive rival returns, on average.[223] The rationale behind the three main hypotheses is supposed to lead to the observed positive wealth effects. Due to the focus on both cross-border acquisitions and a European set of rivals, the market power hypothesis is expected to be of minor importance here, especially for the earlier years. In contrast, particularly efficiency considerations as well as expectations of increased acquisition probability (to a limited extent) are expected to be the main drivers of returns. In line with the findings and arguments of Eckbo (1983), it is expected that anticipated future efficiency gains at rival banks outweigh possible negative effects of increased competition.[224] Effects under the Efficiency Hypothesis are therefore supposed to lead to positive

---

223   In their analysis of rival effects in the banking industry, Campa/Hernando (2005) do not find significant abnormal returns. However, as this is the only study yielding this result and as a simple mean return model is employed to calculate excess returns, this thesis takes a different view. Moreover, in contrast to their expectation that any rival effects will occur within national borders, the author believes that the impact of an M&A announcement also goes across borders (particularly in Europe).

224   Cf. Eckbo (1983), p. 245–269.

reactions at competitors due to anticipated future efficiency spill-over. In accordance with this argument, Altunbaz/Ibanez (2004) find that in the case of cross-border M&A, the performance of banks in the European Union improves.[225] In combination with a limited increase of acquisition probability, these arguments lead to hypothesis 2.

Hypothesis 2)   The announcement leads to positive abnormal returns for European rival banks.

While rival returns are expected to be positive, on average, , there should be a difference in returns regarding the regional proximity of target and competitor. Increasing proximity to the acquired target should lead to stronger effects under all three rival hypotheses. Changes in the competitive balance of the industry should be most prevalent near the location of the target. As domestic banking markets still differ along many dimensions in Europe, effects should be strongest within national borders. Recent European evidence underlines these arguments. Bley/Madura (2003) have shown that positive rival effects of M&A announcements weaken with geographic distance from the target.[226] Findings indicated that the observed positive abnormal returns are larger for rivals that are located in the same country as the target than for competitors located in another European country.

This proximity effect should be similarly applicable (although possibly in weaker form) for geographic regions of closely related countries, such as the Benelux countries or Scandinavia. Ties between countries in such regions are stronger both in economic as well as cultural terms. As a result there could be a proximity effect that stretches beyond domestic borders yet predominantly stays within regions. The author assumes proximity effects to not stop at borders and remain domestic, but instead expects rival effects to vary more flexibly with proximity to the targets across borders. These arguments lead to a broader definition of hypothesis 3:

Hypothesis 3)   Rival effects increase with regional proximity to the target.

Chapter III.2 has shown that considerable efforts have been undertaken within the Single Market Program to integrate European markets in order to foster the creation of a single European market. As the process is still occurring, it can be said that major achievements have already been made – the creation of a single

---

225   Cf. Altunbas/Ibanez (2004), p. 6.
226   Cf. Bley/Madura (2003), p. 382.

currency probably being the most important and prominent example. As the individual markets have therefore grown together to some extent, European countries should be closer to each other (along several dimensions) as compared to non-EU countries. The market should thus view it differently, whether a European or a non-European bidder makes an acquisition in the EU. On one side, arguments under the market power hypothesis indicate that rival effects should be more profound for EU acquirers. On the other side, arguments under the efficiency hypothesis rather point towards possibly increased positive spill-over effects in the case of non-EU bidders. Under this argument, rival returns should be higher when the acquirer is not from the EU. Effects under the acquisition probability hypothesis are unclear. As prior evidence could not validate the market power hypothesis and as European banking markets are still only concentrated on a domestic level, efficiency spill-over considerations should dominate rival effects regarding the location of the bidder. This leads to hypothesis 4.

Hypothesis 4)   Rival returns are higher when the bidder is located outside the EU.

Table III.2 provides an overview of the proposed hypotheses.

Table III.2: Overview of Hypotheses

1a	The announcement has an abnormal negative effect on bidder share price.
1b	The announcement has an abnormal positive effect on target share price.
2	The announcement leads to positive abnormal returns for European rival banks.
3	Rival effects increase with regional proximity to the target.
4	Rival returns are higher when the bidder is located outside the EU.

Source: Personal Summary.

III.4 Event Study Analysis

III.4.1 Applied Methodology

III.4.1.1 Market Model and Abnormal Returns

As mentioned before, event study methodology is employed to assess whether there are any abnormal value effects as a result of cross-border M&A announcements in the European banking industry. Event study methodology has been ap-

80

plied in a large body of scientific research[227] as it yields a reliable measure of the value created (or destroyed) by the announcement of an envisaged M&A transaction. The event study approach is therefore a suitable as well as the standard methodology to assess the type of research questions at hand. In a first step, I assess the abnormal effects of acquisition announcements on both bidder and target shareholder value, which is similar to the chosen approach of most prior research. In a second step, I broaden the analysis on effects of the same M&A announcements on European banking rivals of the target.

As markets are assumed to be informational efficient[228], the information signal that comes from the announcement of the M&A transaction will disseminate quickly in the marketplace.[229] If arrival of this new information then changes the market view about bidder and/or target involved in the announced transaction as well as the market view on competing banks, then their prices should correctly reflect this restatement of expectations. As a result, abnormal returns can usually be exhibited around the announcement of an M&A transaction.

Because of the wide spread application of event studies, there are numerous different methods for the individual steps. Peterson (1989) already stated that there is no such thing as a standard event study methodology.[230] The following therefore describes the specific methodology approach chosen for this study.

I have applied the market model put forward by Dodd/Warner (1983) and Brown/Warner (1985)[231] to calculate expected returns R_{jt} for stock j at time t:

(1) $$R_{jt} = \alpha_j + \beta_j R_{mt} + \varepsilon_{jt}$$

where: R_{jt} return of stock j on day t

            R_{mt} market return on day t

α_j intercept
β_j coefficient
ε_{jt} error term

OLS-regressions for each individual stock are applied over the estimation period with stocks being the dependent and the respective market indices the explaining variable in order to calculate regression intercept α_j and coefficient β_j.

227 Cf. Khotari/Warner (2004), p. 4.
228 In the semi-strong form.
229 Cf. Fama (1976), p. 383–417, and Fama (1970), p. 143–145.
230 Cf. Peterson (1989), p. 36.
231 Cf. Dodd/Warner (1983), p. 401–438, and Brown/Warner (1985), p. 3–31.

Intercept and coefficient are then used to calculate expected returns from the observed market returns during the event window:

(2) $\quad E(R_{jt}) = \alpha_j + \beta_j R_{mt}$

where: $\quad$ E (R_{jt}) $\quad$ expected return of stock j on day t

This expected return is then subtracted from the observed stock return, which yields the abnormal return AR_{jt} of stock j on day t.

(3) $\quad AR_{jt} = R_{jt} - E(R_{jt})$

In the next step abnormal returns are aggregated (summed up) over the event window(s) to give the cumulated abnormal return $CAR_{j\,[t1;\,t2]}$ for each of n stocks in the sample.

(4) $\quad CAR_{j[t_1;t_2]} = \sum_{t_1}^{t_2} AR_{jt}$

Finally, the CARs are aggregated over the stocks and divided by n to yield the cumulated average abnormal return CAAR $_{[t1;\,t2]}$ of the group.[232]

(5) $\quad CAAR_{[t_1;t_2]} = \frac{1}{n} \cdot \sum_{j}^{n} CAR_{j[t_1;t_2]}$

Finally, test statistics determine the statistical significance of the observed CAARs. The Boehmer-Test[233] is applied in this study, as this is the only test statistic which explicitly accounts for a possible variance increase during the event period and thereby leads to more robust results than other test statistics.[234] In addition, mean difference tests check for significance of CAAR differences between the sub-samples.

---

232 The same aggregation process is conducted for the individual competitors included in the rival portfolio.
233 Cf. Boehmer/Musumeci/Poulsen (1991), p. 253–272.
234 Cf. Sera (2002), p. 6.

III.4.1.2 Event Window Selection

The event window should be long enough so that all share price reactions related to the transaction announcement can be captured. On the other hand, the event window should be kept short in order not to include any confounding effects.[235] Within this study, an event window T of 41 days: T = [–20; +20] (where t = {0} denominates the announcement date of a transaction) is considered, wherein the returns of 20 trading days prior to 20 days after the announcement are analyzed. To get more detailed results, CAARs for the following sub-event windows are also being calculated: [–20;0], [–5;0], {0}, [–1;1], [0;5], [0;20].

To estimate the model parameters intercept α_j and coefficient β_j needed in the expected return calculations, an estimation period of between 100 to 300 days can be chosen.[236] This study applies an estimation period consisting of 200 days. Figure III.1 illustrates the estimation period and event window selection of this study.

Figure III.1: Estimation Period and Event Window Selection

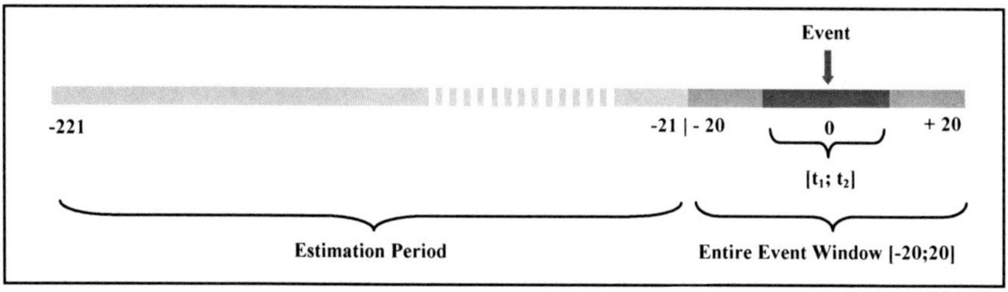

Source: Personal design concurring with Peterson (1989), p. 38.

III.4.2 Sample and Data Selection

To identify relevant M&A transactions, Thomson Financial SDC (Securities Data Company – M&A Database) is used as the prime data source. Stock and index[237] returns were provided by Datastream, which is another database from Thomson Financial. Relevant transactions were selected according to the following criteria:

235   Cf. McWilliams/Siegel (1997), p. 636.
236   Cf. Peterson (1989), p. 38.
237   For the analysis of bidder and target returns, regional MSCI indices were applied in the market model regressions. For US bidders, the S&P 500 composite index was used. All regressions for the rival portfolio were based on the MSCI Europe index.

- The transaction was announced between January 1, 1990 and December 31, 2005.
- The acquired target is a bank located in the old EU-15 or Norway and Switzerland.[238]
- The acquirer is from a different country than the target.
- Transaction volume exceeded €100 million.
- Target or bidder were exchange listed at announcement.
- A change of corporate control has occurred during the transaction (>50% only after transaction).
- Deal status is completed.

This SDC request yielded a deal list of 103 transactions. However, the list shortened considerably as in some transactions the target was not truly a bank, but rather an asset- or loan portfolio. Moreover, some deals were of domestic nature instead of being cross-border. And finally, some stocks didn't show enough liquidity, i.e. price movements. As a result, 52 transactions were eliminated and the final deal list shortened to 51 cross-border M&A transactions in the European banking industry between 1990 and 2005. As expected, the number of cross-border acquisitions in Europe's banking industry was rather small over that period.

However, the data sample for the main analysis is quite large, as the effects of the 51 transaction announcements are not only applied to bidders and targets. A key element of this study is to broaden the analysis of announcement effects upon European rival banks of the targets. To identify the applicable competing banks for the construction of rival portfolios, the national Datastream banking indices were used.[239] Downloading constituent lists for all countries resulted in 17 lists of European Banks, one for each country in this study's geographic area of analysis. After accounting for lack of liquidity (i.e. price movements) of the shares of 14 banks, a total of 122 banks is included in the rival portfolio.

Table III.3 provides an overview of the regional distribution of competing firms, which constitute the total rival portfolio.

---

238 This geographic focus resembles the old EU plus nearby Switzerland and Norway. It is similar to other studies. Cf. e.g. Beitel/Lorenz/Schiereck (2005).
239 The constituent lists of Datastream's own indices are denominated by the industry-specific Mnemonic code "LBANKS" plus a two-digit country suffix. E.g., the constituent list for Denmark is denominated by "LBANKSDK".

Table III.3: Geographic Distribution of Total Rival Portfolio

Country No.	Country	No. of Rival Banks
1	Austria	2
2	Belgium	5
3	Denmark	6
4	Finland	1
5	France	8
6	Germany	7
7	Greece	11
8	Ireland	3
9	Italy	26
10	Luxemburg	1
11	Netherlands	3
12	Norway	2
13	Portugal	5
14	Spain	14
15	Sweden	4
16	Switzerland	15
17	UK	9
Total		122

Source: Datastream.

III.4.3 Descriptive Statistics

The final transaction sample consists of 51 cross-border M&A acquisitions that occurred in the European banking industry from 1990 to 2005. Within these 51 M&A transactions, 42 bidders and 17 targets were both publicly listed and additionally exhibited sufficient liquidity. The limited number of listed targets is due to the fact that most targets were previously either government owned or subsidiaries of a larger banking institution and were thus not publicly traded. Concerning the regional distribution of the directly involved banks, as defined in the SDC request, all targets were located in one of the 17 defined European countries. The largest number of targets acquired in a single country was a total of ten banks located in Europe's largest economy, namely Germany, followed by the UK and Spain, each with six banks being acquired. During our sample period, no single bank in Ireland or Luxemburg was purchased.

Concerning the group of bidders, 45 banks were located within the EU and thereby fostered intra-European integration of the banking industry. Only six acquirers were located outside of Europe, with two bidders each coming from Iceland and the US. Interestingly, the largest single number of bidders came from Swedish banks, which made a total of seven acquisitions, followed by French and German banks that engaged in six transactions each. Table III.4 provides an overview of the regional distribution of both bidders and targets.

Table III.4: Geographic Distribution of Bidders and Targets

Region	Country	Bidders	Targets
Europe	Austria	0	2
	Belgium	2	4
	Denmark	3	3
	Finland	0	1
	France	6	4
	Germany	6	10
	Greece	0	1
	Ireland	1	0
	Italy	3	2
	Luxemburg	2	0
	Netherlands	5	4
	Norway	0	5
	Portugal	1	1
	Spain	2	6
	Sweden	7	1
	Switzerland	2	1
	United Kingdom	5	6
	Subtotal	45	51
Other	Australia	1	
	Iceland	2	
	South Africa	1	
	United States	2	
	Subtotal	6	0
Total		51	51

Source: Thomson SDC.

With regard to M&A occurrence over time, yearly transactions' numbers and volumes vary widely. Unexpectedly, the bulk of deals did not occur in recent years. Transactions are rather spread out over the entire sample period. Figure III.2 illustrates the number of transactions and transaction volume in the sample period by year.

Figure III.2: Number of Transactions and Volume over Time

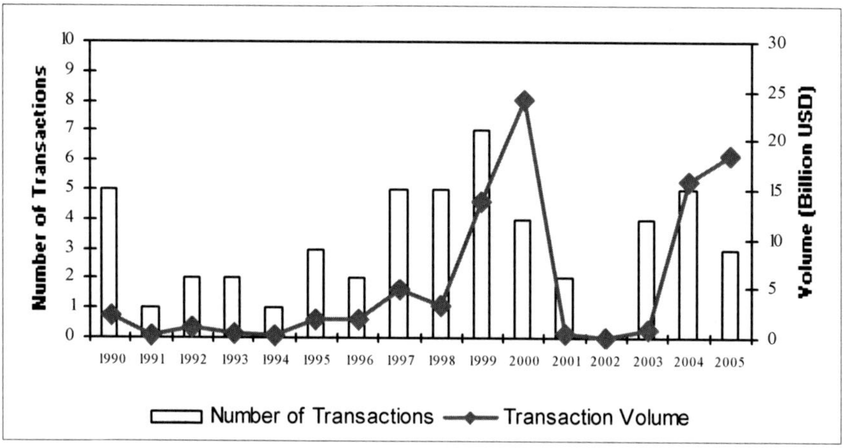

As figure III.2 illustrates, the year 1990 already showed strong cross-border M&A activity with five transactions, followed by rather weak years until cross-border consolidation picked up strongly in 1997 and 1998. The year 1999 marked the peak in terms of transactions numbers with seven acquisitions taking place. Deal occurrence then declined until the year 2002 in which not a single acquisition happened. From 2003 until present, cross-border M&A activity in Europe's banking industry has picked up again. This is particularly true concerning transaction volume. Whereas average deal size has been rather small in the early and mid 1990s, this changed considerably with the boom of capital markets at the end of the last century. Transaction volume jumped in 1999 and reached its all-time peak in the year 2000 when price-earnings (P/E) ratios at capital markets were the highest (before equity prices started to plunge again in the second half of the year). Accordingly, transaction volume was rather low in 2001 and 2003 but picked up considerably in 2004 and 2005. This was mainly due to two landmark transactions: The acquisition of Abbey National by Banco Santander for €12.995

billion in 2004 and the largest cross-border banking acquisition until now in Europe, between Unicredito and HVB for €15.073 billion in 2005.

According to the data sample, acquiring banks are more than four times larger than target banks.[240] The average (mean) market capitalization of listed banks at the announcement day amounts to $18.618 billion for the group of bidders and $4.472 billion for the group of targets.[241] The maximum and the minimum transaction rank value amount to €15.073 billion and €108 million, respectively, with an average rank value within the transaction sample of €1.564 billion.[242] This is also the average acquisition price bidders had to pay. Clearly, this number is driven upwards by the large transactions of the years 1999, 2000, 2004, and 2005.

III.4.4 Event Study Results

III.4.4.1 Bidders and Targets

In the aggregate, I find a value destruction of $10.450 billion during the three-day interval surrounding the announcement for the group of listed bidders, which is mainly driven by some large acquirers accumulating significant losses.[243] The group of listed targets exhibits an aggregate value generation of $6.162 billion over the same interval. This implies that for the combined entity value, the amount of $4.378 billion was destroyed. However, as returns and market capitalization figures for only 17 targets are available compared to availability of these numbers for 42 acquirers, this calculation yields a misleading perspective. When calculating the combined entity view with average value generation/destruction figures of all transactions in our sample, I find an average value generation of $111 million per deal or $5.688 billion in the aggregate for the combined entity. This implies that, on average, cross-border deals in Europe's banking industry have been value creating for the combined entity.[244]

---

240 Please note that these figures are biased, as only listed entities are reflected.
241 Market capitalization figures are denoted in USD, as before the introduction of the Euro exchange rates in the year 1998, there are no "market caps" available on Datastream, which are denoted in Euro. However, most M&A studies in the literature use USD as well.
242 Rank value figures denoted in Euro were provided by Thomson Financial SDC.
243 Again, these figures are biased, as only listed entities are reflected.
244 If calculations weren't driven by a few large deals in which acquirers accumulated significant losses, the combined entity view would be considerably more positive.

Figure III.3 illustrates the development of the cumulated average abnormal return of both bidders and targets over the entire event window. Interestingly, in contrast to prior research and hypothesis 1a bidder shareholders do not experience (small) negative returns.[245] Instead, they exhibit a small positive revaluation of their shares, which grows steadily over the entire event window. Target shareholders enjoy a considerable positive revaluation of their shares, as expected. Although parts of the positive returns already develop before the announcement, the largest reevaluation occurs in a three day interval surrounding the announcement of the transaction.

Figure III.3: CAAR Development over the entire Event Window

Cumulated Average Abnormal Return (CAAR) [-20;+20]

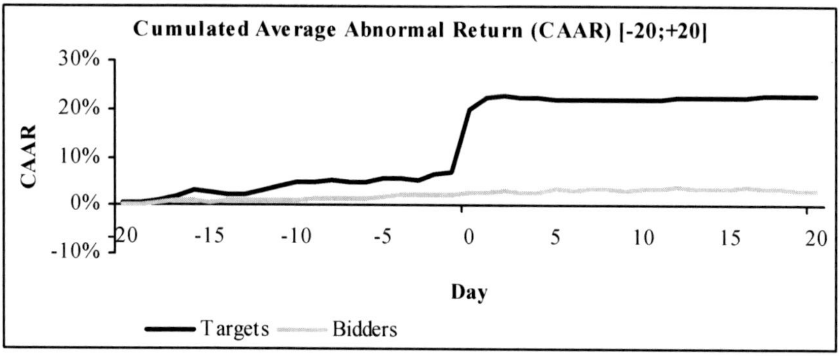

Source: Personal calculations; data: Datastream.

Table III.5 provides a more comprehensive view of the returns for both bidders and targets. It illustrates the exact CAARs for the seven event windows as well as the corresponding test statistics. Similarly, as figure III.3 shows, table III.5 underlines that acquirers, on average, enjoy small positive CAARs in all event windows, with the largest value generation of 3.06% accruing over the entire event window. However, despite returns being positive in all event windows, none of the CAARs are significantly different from zero. Instead, p-values are all above at least 0.5 due to the wide dispersion of results (including large negative returns for some of the large bidders). For the group of targets, CAARs are large and positive over all event windows. Over the entire event window [–20;20], tar-

---

245   Please note that in absolute terms, value was destroyed on aggregate for the group of bidders as outlined before. However, as this is driven by some large acquirers, accumulating significant losses the return based analysis yields slight positive results, on average (driven by many smaller bidders accumulating positive returns).

get shareholders enjoy a positive revaluation of their shares in the amount of 22.86%, which is significant at the 1%-level. All other CAARs, which vary between 12.98% and 19.75%, are positive at a significance level of 10% and at a level of 5% for the [–20;0] event window. In the three day interval surrounding the announcement day (event window [–1;1]), bidders and targets experience CAARs of 0.51% and 16.16%, respectively.

Table III.5: CAARs of Bidders and Targets

Bidders				Targets			
N=44	**CAAR**	**P-Value**	**Sig.**	**N=17**	**CAAR**	**P-Value**	**Sig.**
[–20;20]	3.06%	0.5110		[–20;20]	22.86%	0.0093	***
[–20;0]	2.42%	0.6965		[–20;0]	19.75%	0.0227	**
[–5;0]	0.86%	0.6137		[–5;0]	14.93%	0.0667	*
{0}	0.34%	0.8743		{0}	12.98%	0.0986	*
[–1;1]	0.51%	0.9360		[–1;1]	16.16%	0.0593	*
[0;5]	1.19%	0.8243		[0;5]	15.03%	0.0674	*
[0;20]	0.97%	0.6058		[0;20]	16.09%	0.0502	*

*Note: ***=significant at 1%-level; **=significant at 5%-level; *=significant at 10%-level.*
Source: Personal calculations; data: Datastream.

III.4.4.2 Rival Effects of Total Rival Portfolio

The total rival portfolio consists of up to 122 individual competing banks that come from the 17 defined European countries.[246] As portfolio composition changes over the years, a number of 68 to 122 rivals entered the calculation for each transaction announcement. Only those rivals were included in the calculations for which full share price data was available for both the 200 days in the estimation period as well as the 41 days in the event window. This resulted in a total number of 5127 rivals for the 51 transactions that constitute the total rival portfolio.[247]

As table III.6 illustrates below, significant rival effects can be observed for the total rival portfolio. Over the entire event window [–20;20], shareholders of European competing banks enjoy a positive revaluation of their shares in the amount of 0.82%, which is highly significant at the 1%-level. Besides the three day interval surrounding the announcement day (event window [–1;1]), all other event windows exhibit positive CAARs, which are significant. Interestingly, on

---

246 Cf. table III.3 for the regional distribution of banks in the total rival portfolio.
247 One single rival bank can be included as many times in the total rival portfolio, as there are M&A announcements in the data sample (i.e. 51 times).

the announcement day (event window {0}), the abnormal return is only 0.02%, which is, however, still significant at the 5%-level given the numerous observations. The largest part of the positive CAAR develops in the 20 days before the announcement. This abnormal return of 0.59% is significant at the 1%-level. Afterwards, starting with the transaction announcement, the following 20 days (event window [0;20]) yield a positive CAAR of 0.26%, which is again significant at the 1%-level.

Table III.6: CAARs of Total Rival Portfolio

Total Rival Portfolio			
N=5127	CAAR	P-Value	Sig.
[–20;20]	0.82%	0.0000	***
[–20;0]	0.59%	0.0000	***
[–5;0]	0.10%	0.0624	*
{0}	0.02%	0.0254	**
[–1;1]	–0.02%	0.2070	
[0;5]	0.06%	0.0016	***
[0;20]	0.26%	0.0000	***

Note: ***=significant at 1%-level; **=significant at 5%-level; *=significant at 10%-level.
Source: Personal calculations; data: Datastream.

III.4.4.3 Rival Effects according to Regional Proximity to Target

To determine whether regional proximity of the competing banks to the location of the target has an influence on rival returns (and thereby test hypothesis 3), the total rival portfolio is divided into domestic and non-domestic rivals. As expected, the two groups experience significantly different CAARs, indicating a clear proximity or "domestic" wealth effects. Table III.7 illustrates the different CAARs of domestic and non-domestic rival banks below.

CAARs of domestic rivals are much larger, amounting to 2.78% over the entire event window [–20;20], compared to 0.72% of non-domestic rivals over the same period. The mean difference test confirms that the difference is not only large, but also significant at the 1%-level for the entire event window. Overall, CAARs of domestic rivals are larger in all event windows and often more significant despite consisting of considerably less observations (317 observations as compared to 4810 for non-domestic rivals). Nevertheless, non-domestic rivals also exhibit positive returns, which are significant in the longer event windows. Considering the mean difference test, CAARs are significantly different over all event windows and particularly for the three day interval surrounding the announcement day. For this event window [−1;1], the CAAR difference amounts to 1.00% and is highly significant above the 1%-level

Table III.7: CAARs of Domestic vs. Non-domestic Rivals

Domestic Rivals			Non-domestic Rivals				Meandifference		
N=317	CAAR	P-Value	Sig.	N=4810	CAAR	P-Value	Sig.	CAAR	P-Value	Sig.
[−20;20]	2.78%	0.0015	***	[−20;20]	0.72%	0.0000	***	2.07%	0.0034	***
[−20;0]	1.61%	0.0804	*	[−20;0]	0.55%	0.0000	***	1.06%	0.0499	**
[−5;0]	0.62%	0.0027	***	[−5;0]	0.05%	0.2515		0.57%	0.0654	*
[0]	0.21%	0.0444	**	[0]	0.01%	0.0809	*	0.20%	0.0699	*
[−1;1]	0.93%	0.0000	***	[−1;1]	−0.07%	0.9127		1.00%	0.0000	***
[0;5]	1.02%	0.0000	***	[0;5]	0.00%	0.0344	**	1.02%	0.0004	***
[0;20]	1.38%	0.0022	***	[0;20]	0.18%	0.0000	***	1.20%	0.0065	***

Note: ***=significant at 1%-level; **=significant at 5%-level; *=significant at 10%-level.
Source: Personal calculations; data: Datastream.

To further test the regional proximity hypothesis, rivals are divided into two additional subgroups: Regional and non-regional competitors. For this analysis, only those 43 transactions are considered in which the target was listed in one of the defined regions.[248] Regions were defined according to apparent cultural and economic proximity of neighboring states, such as the Benelux countries or Scandinavia. Interestingly, differences between regional and non-regional rivals are not nearly as severe as the domestic and non-domestic sub-samples. Table III.8 below illustrates CAARs of regional and non-regional rivals.

As table III.8 shows above, mean differences are only significant for the three event windows {0}, [−1;1], and [0;5]. However, these differences are comparably large for such short periods, amounting to 0.18% for the announcement day alone and 0.67% for the three-day interval [−1;1]. These differences are significant at the 5%- and 1%-level, respectively. Regional rivals also generally exhibit larger positive CAARs as compared to the non-regional rivals, which are all highly significant at the 1%level (besides the 0.58% CAARs of event window [0;20], which is still significant at the 5%-level). CAARs of non-regional competitors are smaller, particularly at and after the announcement day and are overall less sig-

---

248 Defined regions are the following: The Benelux countries, Austria and Germany, Scandinavia, Spain and Portugal, and, lastly, UK and Ireland.

nificant, despite again consisting of more observations (3917 observations as compared to 436 for regional rivals).[249]

Table III.8: CAARs of Regional vs. Non-regional Rivals

Regional Rivals				Non-Regional Rivals				Meandifference		
N=436	CAAR	P-Value	Sig.	N=3917	CAAR	P-Value	Sig.	CAAR	P-Value	Sig.
[−20;20]	1.10%	0.0010	***	[−20;20]	0.96%	0.0000	***	0.14%	0.7911	
[−20;0]	0.73%	0.0060	***	[−20;0]	0.76%	0.0000	***	−0.03%	0.9333	
[−5;0]	0.34%	0.0059	***	[−5;0]	0.03%	0.4171		0.31%	0.1338	
[0]	0.21%	0.0033	***	[0]	0.03%	0.0633	*	0.18%	0.0223	**
[−1;1]	0.58%	0.0000	***	[−1;1]	−0.09%	0.4770		0.67%	0.0000	***
[0;5]	0.55%	0.0003	***	[0;5]	0.03%	0.0246	**	0.52%	0.0043	***
[0;20]	0.58%	0.0146	**	[0;20]	0.23%	0.0000	***	0.35%	0.3079	

*Note: ***=significant at 1%-level; **=significant at 5%-level; *=significant at 10%-level.*
Source: Personal calculations; data: Datastream.

III.4.4.4 Rival Effects according to Location of Bidder

To determine whether the location of the bidder has an effect on rival returns, the sample is divided into two types of transactions: Acquisitions where the bidder is from one of the 17 defined European countries, and transactions where the bidder is based in another country. As table III.4 in section III.4.3 already showed, six bidders were located in another country and 45 were located inside the old EU-15 or Norway and Switzerland.

Table III.9 illustrates the rival CAARs according to bidder region.

As table III.9 shows, rival CAARs for EU bidder transactions are quite dispersed and vary from insignificant −0.04% for the three-day interval to 0.79% for the entire event window [−20;20], which is highly significant at the 1%-level. Similarly, the positive CAARs of the event windows [−20;0], [0;5], and [0;20] are significant at the 1%-level. Considering rival returns when the bidder was from outside the defined EU, results are considerably less significant. Although CAARs are generally slightly larger for this sub- sample (due to less and dispersed observations), only the event windows [−20;20] and [0;5] exhibit abnormal returns, which are significant (at the 5%-level). Accordingly, the mean dif-

---

249 The total number of observations is smaller here, as some transactions included a target which was not located in one of the defined regions. These transactions were thus not included in the analysis at this point.

ference tests overall yield no significant results. Only the CAARs of the event window [0;5] are significantly different from zero (at the 10%-level).

Table III.9: Rival CAARs according to Bidder Region

EU Bidders				Non-EU Bidders				Meandifference		
N=4509	CAAR	P-Value	Sig.	N=618	CAAR	P-Value	Sig.	CAAR	P-Value	Sig.
[−20;20]	0.79%	0.0000	***	[−20;20]	1.06%	0.0770	*	−0.27%	0.6343	
[−20;0]	0.55%	0.0000	***	[−20;0]	0.88%	0.1024		−0.33%	0.4422	
[−5;0]	0.08%	0.1008		[−5;0]	0.25%	0.3661		−0.17%	0.4906	
[0]	0.00%	0.0519	*	[0]	0.11%	0.2389		−0.11%	0.1623	
[−1;1]	−0.04%	0.2046		[−1;1]	0.13%	0.8314		−0.17%	0.2358	
[0;5]	0.02%	0.0069	***	[0;5]	0.34%	0.0721	*	−0.32%	0.0745	*
[0;20]	0.25%	0.0000	***	[0;20]	0.29%	0.2950		−0.04%	0.9002	

*Note: ***=significant at 1%-level; **=significant at 5%-level; *=significant at 10%-level.*
Source: Personal calculations; data: Datastream.

III.4.5 Discussion

Concurrent with prior research outlined in section III.3.1 as well as expectations under hypothesis 1a, returns for the group of bidders are found to be insignificant over all seven event windows. For the shareholders of acquiring banks, M&A transactions do not create wealth, but neither do they destroy value. From their perspective, cross-border acquisitions can rather be viewed as a zero sum game. In contrast, the abnormal returns for the group of targets are highly positive beyond expectations (under hypothesis 1b as well as from results from prior research). CAARs of almost 23% over the entire event window are extraordinarily large. Despite abnormal returns being significant, this finding should be viewed with caution, as only 17 targets were publicly listed and therefore entered the calculations. This number of observations is too small to draw any far-reaching conclusions for CAARs at banking targets in general. Nevertheless, these high abnormal target returns within cross-border M&A could be an indication that defensive actions of regulators and/or governments or national bidders have driven up premiums considerably. It seems that foreign bidders needed to pay more in order to gain control (as compared to domestic bidders). In this respect, it is surprising that bidders did not destroy value for their own shareholders by engaging in these costly transactions.

Interestingly, value is created for the combined entity, on average, by the observed transactions. Although the number of observations is small, results indicate considerable wealth increases of an average of more than $100 million per transaction. Cross-border M&A transactions thus are to be viewed positively in the aggregate as they generally create value. The combined entity appears to be worth more than the sum of the parts previously. The market thus seems to have a positive view on cross-border transactions within Europe's banking industry and values them accordingly.

Consistent with most prior research and expectations under hypothesis 2, the analysis yields significant positive abnormal returns for the entire European rival bank portfolio. Despite differences in European domestic banking markets and a still limited level of intra-European integration, significant effects for the total portfolio can be observed. This is an indication that rival effects in the banking industry are not limited to stay within domestic borders as proposed by Campa and Hernando (2005),[250] but instead can be observed on an international level at competing banks all across Europe. Another possible explanation is that, to some degree, these 17 European countries could be viewed as a particularly interlinked market by many investors and thereby seem to be more integrated already than originally anticipated. It is important to note that CAARs of e.g. 0.82% for the entire event window are quite large, especially when considering that up to 122 rival banks across Europe are each enjoying this value gain (in each transaction). About two-thirds of this value gain accrues before the announcement of the transaction, which implies that rumors of an impending acquisition seem to have spread before public notification and have driven up prices in the industry, accordingly. Nevertheless, after the announcement, the raised prices not only stabilize, but even rise an additional 0.26% in the following 20 trading days. It is questionable, however, why anticipation of an expected acquisition did not lead to the same effects for both targets and bidders. One possible explanation could be that the market was uncertain which banks would be involved and thus only priced expectations with according probabilities.

It is interesting and important to note at this point that both targets and their rivals benefit significantly from an acquisition. Bidders who engage the transactions in the first place, who should theoretically be following value maximizing strategies, in contrast, do not experience significant positive returns. Results indicate that value is only created for targets and competitors.

Concerning the source of the value gain at rival banks, it seems unlikely that arguments under the market power hypothesis lead to this development, as the European banking markets remains fragmented on a pan-European level. Arguments under the acquisition probability hypothesis could, however, explain part of the value gain; 51 transactions observed over 16 years could very well in-

---

250   Cf. Campa/Hernando (2005), p. 11.

crease the probability of an acquisition of the banks included in the rival portfolio. Nevertheless, as there are a large number of banks left in the market on a pan-European basis, it seems that anticipated efficiency spill-over effects are the main drivers of the value gain. Following this reasoning, cross-border M&A in Europe's banking industry should be viewed positively, as they seem to raise efficiency levels of the industry as a whole. Europe's banking industry thereby benefits from cross-border M&A by exhibiting improvements in performance in the aggregate. This argument is concurrent with the findings of Altunbas and Ibanez (2004), as mentioned in section III.3.3, who report this relationship as being particularly strong for European cross-border M&A.[251] Accordingly, cross-border acquisitions seem to improve performance of Europe's banking industry as a whole and make it more robust through increased competitive strength.

As expected under hypothesis 3 and consistent with prior evidence, the analysis further indicates a significant regional proximity effect on rival returns. Particularly, shareholders of domestic rivals exhibit a much larger positive abnormal return in the amount of 2.78% over the entire event window as compared to 0.72% for non-domestic rival banks over the same period. Moreover, the observed shareholder wealth effects at competing banks of the two sub-samples differ significantly in all event windows. Changes in the competitive balance of the industry indeed seem to be much stronger near the location of the target. While collusion arguments might have limited applicability here since bidding banks are entering a foreign market through their acquisition, the anticipated efficiency spill-over effects are particularly expected to be the main source of the value gain at domestic rivals. Furthermore, domestic rivals could be viewed as attractive additional takeover candidates by market participants, thereby leading to an increased acquisition probability of these banks, which ultimately results in higher share prices.

Interestingly, the supplementary analysis of the regional and the non-regional rival portfolios provides additional confirmation of the regional proximity hypothesis. Rival banks within the region exhibit slightly higher abnormal returns as compared to competing banks located outside the geographic region of the target. With decreasing proximity, effects also seem to be less direct and vary more widely. Although returns for the regional rival portfolio are much smaller than for the domestic portfolio and mean differences are only significant in three of the seven event windows, there is still a measurable difference in rival effects. This is an indication that positive rival effects are indeed greatest near the location of the target and, moreover, weaken with increasing geographic distance from it. As

---

251 Cf. Altunbas/Ibanez (2004), p. 6.

proposed under the regional proximity hypothesis, this effect goes beyond national borders and affects international competitors as well.

As positive rival effects are higher near the target's location and particularly in its home country, the perception on foreign entry in the banking industry needs to be reassessed. Importantly, these positive returns seem not to derive from collusion, but instead mostly from anticipated future efficiency spill-over effects. This implies a positive and lasting effect which is particularly strong for the domestic banking industry. Through foreign entry, competing banks seem to become more efficient over the medium term, thereby strengthening the national banking industry as a whole. In light of this evidence, regulators and governments should not deter foreign bidders, but rather welcome them.

Expectations on differences of shareholder wealth effects at rival banks (depending on the geographic location of the bidder) are not supported by the results. Although abnormal returns at competing banks are slightly higher in the case of non-EU bidder acquisitions, results are generally not significant as they are too dispersed. The lack of statistical significance in the mean difference test confirms this view. It seems that there is no strict relationship between rival returns and the location of the bidder. However, results could also be that widely dispersed, as there are only a small number of non-EU bidder transactions. In addition, the six bidders are located in four very different regions of the world, which probably led to diverse assessments of the individual transactions.

Table III.10 summarizes the results with respect to the proposed hypotheses.

Table III.10: Overview of Hypotheses Confirmation

1a	The announcement has an abnormal negative effect on bidder share price.	rejected
1b	The announcement has an abnormal positive effect on target share price.	confirmed
2	The announcement leads to positive abnormal returns for European rival banks.	confirmed
3	Rival effects increase with regional proximity to the target.	confirmed
4	Rival returns are higher when the bidder is located outside the EU.	rejected

Source: Personal summary.

III.5 Conclusion

An unprecedented level of consolidation activity has been reshaping Europe's banking industry since the early 1990s. The bulk of M&A activity, however, occurred within national borders, which left the banking industry fragmented on a pan-European basis. As most domestic markets are already quite concentrated, banking institutions will increasingly have to look across borders to find suitable acquisition candidates. Until recently, cross-border acquisitions were viewed with criticism as there seemed to be a lack of a beneficial economic rationale for this type of transaction. The still-limited prior research on European banking M&A generally confirms this view. But perceptions are changing and cross-border acquisitions are believed to increasingly be able to create value. Additionally, national regulators and governments who traditionally tried to fend off acquisition proposals of foreign bidders (because domestic banking industries were feared to be threatened by the new entrants) are assumed to be less able to carry out their protectionist actions.

The present study adds empirical evidence to the discussion and clarifies the negative prejudice on cross-border M&A for domestic banking markets. It shows that both domestic and other European rival banks need to be included in the analysis in order to provide a comprehensive assessment of the full effects of M&A on the banking industry. The study analyzes the effects of 51 cross-border M&A transactions in the European banking industry on both bidders and targets as well as on a large portfolio of rivals in all European countries that are included in the dataset.

Results indicate that the negative prejudice on cross-border M&A is unjustified. Whereas bidders experience insignificant returns, target shareholders enjoy a large and significant revaluation of their shares in the amount of almost 23% over the entire event window. For the combined entity, value is, on average, generated.

Effects on rival banks and thereby the industry as a whole should be viewed even more positively. The total portfolio of European rivals exhibits significant small positive abnormal returns of 0.82%. This positive effect grows with increasing proximity to the location of the target. As a result, the group of domestic rivals enjoys significant positive returns of almost 3%. Importantly, these positive effects are not expected to derive from collusion, but instead mostly from anticipated future efficiency spill-over effects. Additionally, an increase in acquisition probability is expected to push up rival share prices. Anticipated future efficiency spill-over effects imply that cross-border M&A have a positive and lasting influence on the European market and most particularly on the domestic banking industry. This renders competing banks more efficient over the medium-term and thereby leads to a more robust national banking industry. In light of this evidence, regulators and governments should not deter foreign bidders, but instead welcome their entry.

In contrast to the above findings, no clear indication was found on the effect of geographic location of the bidder. This could, however, also be due to a limited number of observations and diverse locations of the bidders, which come from outside the EU.

It will be interesting to observe the expected acceleration of cross-border M&A activity in Europe's financial industry in the coming years. As main obstacles seem to be disappearing, these transactions should increasingly generate value as long as managers are mainly pursuing value maximizing goals. The expected growing number of cross-border acquisitions in the European banking industry provides an interesting possibility for further analysis. A larger data sample could provide more meaningful data on both bidders and targets. Moreover, an in-depth analysis of other possible value drivers, such as bidder size or concentration ratios, could deepen the understanding of rival effects. Finally, comparing e.g. domestic and cross-border as well as horizontal and vertical M&A event study results would also allow a clearer allocation of the observed rival effects to the three main hypotheses. It could also be interesting to take the opposite approach and calculate the negative effects of protectionist actions on the banking industry.

IV Shareholder Wealth Effects of REIT M&A: An International Analysis

Abstract

The REIT industry has experienced significant consolidation since the early 1990s and continues to change rapidly through mergers and acquisitions. But are these transactions creating value for the respective shareholders? Interestingly, despite ongoing consolidation activity and despite the sheer size as well as the importance of the industry, hardly any empirical research has analyzed the value implications of REIT M&A. The few existing studies suffer from small sample sizes and do not cover recent years. As a consequence, the question still remains whether REIT M&A do create value for the target as well as for the bidding firms' shareholders.

This paper aims to fill this research gap by assessing the value implications of a large sample of 107 international M&A transactions amongst REITs between the years 1990 and 2005. The analysis uses event study methodology and applies the market model to compute expected returns.

Results indicate that target shareholders, on average, experience a significant positive revaluation of their shares whereas negative wealth effects for bidding firms' shareholders are small and insignificant. In addition, it appears that target status and market sentiment have an influence on size and direction of the observed announcement effects.

IV.1 Introduction

IV.1.1 Objective and Motivation

Real Estate Investment Trusts are an often discussed topic these days. In Germany, the debate is so heated that the German magazine "Going Public" this year devoted an entire issue to the discussion on the proposed introduction of a REIT regime in Germany.[252] The REIT concept has become this popular because in recent years a growing number of nations has successfully introduced own REIT regimes. As a result, the REIT idea is generally becoming more widespread in the

---

252 Cf. Going Public, March 2006.

world. A typical REIT is thereby understood as a corporation which generates most of its revenues from real estate assets and mortgages.[253] Most importantly, a qualified REIT is exempt from corporate taxes as long as around 80 to 100% of its earnings are distributed to shareholders.[254] Through this beneficial structure, investors can avoid double taxation at both personal and corporate levels. Besides being an attractive indirect real estate investment possibility for investors, REITs also provide an interesting possibility for larger companies to get real estate portfolios out of their books and bring these assets to the market.[255] REIT structures can thereby fulfill important market functions as they provide liquidity for otherwise illiquid real estate assets.

The number of national REIT markets is growing, and particularly the US and the Australian market have grown to considerable size. The US REIT market is the largest and most mature with an aggregate market capitalization of about $330 billion.[256] Presently, an increasing number of nations, e.g. Germany, Malaysia and Taiwan, are considering the introduction of an own REIT regime in their respective local markets.[257] The UK has introduced an own REIT regime in January 2007.[258]

In contrast to the growing interest in and the numerous discussions on REITs, empirical research has rather had its focus on other areas of interest. Despite the long history of REITs since the introduction in 1960 in the US, a large amount of capital invested in REIT assets and a growing number of nations introducing a REIT regime or considering it, empirical research on REITs has been rather limited until present. This is particularly true, if compared to research on the related banking industry.[259] This lack of prior research is even more surprising as the REIT industry has been subject to significant consolidation activity in the 1990s[260] and as the data of this study shows in more recent years as well. Of course, these numerous acquisitions raise questions on the size and direction of wealth effects for the involved shareholders, which might be caused by these transactions. However, existing research focusing explicitly on M&A (in the REIT industry) is rather limited as well.[261] There are only six relevant studies,

---

253 Cf. Li/Elayan/Meyer (2001), p. 116.
254 Cf. Maris/Elayan (1990), p. 22.
255 Cf. BVI (2006), p. 79.
256 Cf. NAREIT (2006), w/p.
257 Cf. Tross/Fröhlich (2006), p. 14.
258 Cf. Drost (2007), p. 21, 24.
259 Cf. Kirchhoff/Schiereck/Mentz (2006), w/p.
260 Cf. Sahin (2005), p. 321.
261 Cf. Li/Elayan/Meyer (2001), p. 115.

which (except for one) all suffer from sample sizes being small.[262] Additionally, all prior studies concentrate on the US market only and thereby neglect the consolidation tendencies in other less mature REIT markets around the world. Finally, there is no empirical evidence covering M&A transactions in the years after 1998 in which the pace of consolidation in REIT markets continued to accelerate.

This study aims to fill this research gap by providing the first study on REIT M&A, which goes beyond the US market and thereby explicitly includes transactions in all global REIT markets. In addition, the time period is extended until the end of 2005, which allows including all transactions of the modern REIT era[263] from the beginning of the 1990s until present. The resulting data set consists of a total of 107 transactions. In the analysis, the following questions are addressed: Do bidder and/or target shareholders gain from M&A in the REIT industry? Are the observed wealth effects different for US- and non-US acquisitions? Do wealth effects change over time? And finally, do acquisitions of private targets yield more positive wealth effects than those of public targets?

To assess the proposed research questions, in accordance with related prior research, an event study is conducted that analyzes share price reactions of both targets and bidders to announcements of M&A transactions in the REIT industry.

IV.1.2 Course of the Investigation

The course of the investigation is structured as follows: First, chapter IV.2 lays out some necessary background knowledge on REITs.[264] Section IV.2.1 provides a descriptive REIT definition as well as a short summary of its main characteristics. From this starting point, the historic development of REITs is outlined. Section IV.2.2 thereby focuses solely on the US market, as the first REIT regime was introduced here. Section IV.2.3 then broadens the historic development to the internationalization of REITs, which began with the introduction of a REIT regime in The Netherlands in 1969 and ends in France in 2003. Section IV.2.4 then concludes the background section by elaborating on some peculiarities of the REIT structure that result from the strict legal requirements, which are applicable particularly in relation to tax status.

In the next step, a literature review of prior research on REIT M&A is provided in section IV.3.1. Based on this review as well as on arguments mentioned

---

262 Cf. section IV.3.1. for an overview of prior research on REIT M&A.
263 Cf. Campbell/Petrova/Sirmans (2003), p. 347.
264 Those familiar with the REIT concept can go directly to section IV.3.

in section IV.2.4, the four hypotheses to be tested in the event study are developed in section IV.3.2.

The event study is then carried out in section IV.4. In a first step, the chosen event study methodology, which includes the selection of the market model, is described in section IV.4.1.1. In a second step, both estimation period and event window selection are described in section IV.4.1.2. Sample and data selection criteria as well as data sources are outlined in section IV.4.2. Descriptive statistics of the data set are presented in section IV.4.3. Finally, section IV.4.4 presents results of the analysis, which are then discussed and interpreted in section IV.4.5.

Section IV.5 wraps up the findings and concludes the essay.

IV.2 Background Knowledge on REITs

IV.2.1 Definition

The term "REIT" is an abbreviated form of the original term "Real Estate Investment Trust" used in US tax legislation.[265] Generally speaking, a REIT is a publicly listable vehicle that has a tax-transparent structure and that (almost) fully distributes earnings to its shareholders.[266] The original idea was to allow private investors to hold portfolios of illiquid real estate assets that through the REIT structure become marketable and liquid investments.[267] Although REITs have slightly different structures depending on national legislation, the REIT concept generally comes down to three constituting elements:[268]

- A REIT primarily invests in real estate assets as well as mortgages.[269] The majority of earnings must stem from real estate.
- A qualified REIT enjoys special tax treatment, which explicitly exempts it from corporate earnings taxes.[270] As a result REIT shareholders can avoid double taxation on both personal and corporate level.
- Third, depending on applicable national regulation, REITs are required to pay out 80 to 100% of earnings to their shareholders each year to retain their special REIT status (corporate tax exemption).[271]

---

265 Cf. Rehkugler (2003), p. 197.
266 Cf. UBS (2004), p. 5.
267 Cf. Zietz/Sirmans/Friday (2003), p.127.
268 Cf. ZEW/ebs (2005), p. 1.
269 Cf. Li/Elayan/Meyer (2001), p. 116.
270 Cf. Maris/Elayan (1990), p. 22.
271 Cf. Campbell/Sirmans (2002), p. 389–390.

Due to the high required earnings payouts amounting sometimes close to 100%, REITs generally have very limited possibilities to accumulate cash for growth strategies.[272] This feature and other specific characteristic (which derive from the legal restrictions imposed on REITs) are being discussed in section 2.4, where further peculiarities resulting from the REIT structure are outlined.

IV.2.2 Historical Development in the US

The history of REITs dates back to 1960, when they were first introduced in the US. As it is also still by far the biggest REIT market globally, the following discussion starts by outlining the historic development of the US REIT industry. In a second step, the discussion will then be broadened to the internationalization of REITs and developments in the respective national markets in chapter 2.3.

As mentioned above, REITs first came into existence in the US in 1960 when the Real Estate Investment Trust Act was passed. The intention of the legislation at that time was to enable small investors to indirectly invest in large real estate portfolios by encouraging the formation of publicly traded real estate corporations.[273] REITs in that sense provide liquidity to otherwise illiquid assets.[274] Market acceptance was good in the following 15 years as the industry grew to a level of total assets amounting to $21.3 billion in 1975.[275] However, during the mid-1970s the industry experienced a series of bankruptcies and liquidations.[276] Main reasons for this development were mismanagement and the extensive use of floating rate financing, which exposed REITs to considerable interest rate risk. In the following ten years, the industry was marked by significant consolidation and it slowly recovered to a level of total assets amounting to almost $17 billion. In reaction to these developments, the first changes in the legal environment of REITs also occurred in the mid-1970s. Amongst other things, REITs were now also allowed to operate as a corporation instead of a trust.

Further important amendments followed with the Tax Reform Act (TRA) in 1986. In the beginning, REITs were structured as a passive investment company, but other than stock or bond portfolios, real estate portfolios require active management of the assets.[277] Until 1986, this active portfolio management had to be

---

272   Cf. Campbell/Ghosh/Sirmans (2001), p. 365.
273   Cf. Flewelling/Spiesbach (1982), p. 256.
274   Cf. Zietz/Sirmans/Friday (2003), p. 127.
275   Cf. Haight/Ford (1987), w/p.
276   For this and the following, cf. McIntosh/Officer/Born (1989), p. 142.
277   Cf. Ambrose/Linneman (2001), p. 141.

done by external advisors, who were rewarded with a management fee.[278] Usually these fees amounted to a maximum of 1.5% of total assets under management or 25% of net earnings, a considerable amount that could not be distributed to shareholders in this structure. The biggest problem was, however, that the fee structures were in most cases not tied to REIT performance and thereby didn't set the right incentives for the external management. This gave rise to agency conflicts.[279]

The TRA abolished the external management restriction in 1986 and from then onwards explicitly allowed REITs to be managed internally. This led to a rapid increase in REITs internalizing management, which not only lowered management costs (and thereby increased available cash outflows), but also reduced conflicts of interest between management and shareholders.[280] Allowing management to be internalized has often been regarded as the main growth driver of the REIT industry in the 1990s as it allowed REITs to become real operating companies that can fully reap the benefits mentioned above.[281]

Other changes made by the TRA, such as significantly smaller depreciation charge possibilities for real estate and less room for discounting of debt capital, additionally helped the REIT industry flourish as it decreased the comparable attractiveness of competing investment forms, namely that of closed-end real estate funds as well as that of direct real estate investments.[282] However, due to the crisis on the US real estate market at the end of the 1980s and beginning of the 1990s, the various changes made by the TRA did not become noticeable in the overall market development until 1992/1993.[283] After that and up until the present, the REIT industry recovered considerably. While the number of listed REITs rose from 142 in 1992 to about 200 in 2005,[284] the industry market cap increased from about $16 billion to more than $330 billion over the same period. Figure IV.1 illustrates the development of the number of REITs in the US and their aggregate market capitalization.

---

278   Cf. Greer/Farrell (1988), p. 22.
279   Cf. Ambrose/Linneman (2001), p. 141.
280   Cf. e.g. Ambrose/Linneman (2001), p. 141, and Graff (2001), p. 99.
281   Cf. King (1998), p. 39.
282   Cf. Väth (1999), p. 228.
283   Cf. ZEW/ebs (2005), p. 7.
284   According to the data sample, there haven been 60 completed acquisitions of REITs targeting listed US REITs over the last 15 years. Taking this into account, a total of at least 100 REITs needs to have been newly listed over that time.

Figure IV.1: Number of REITs in the US (composite) and Market Cap

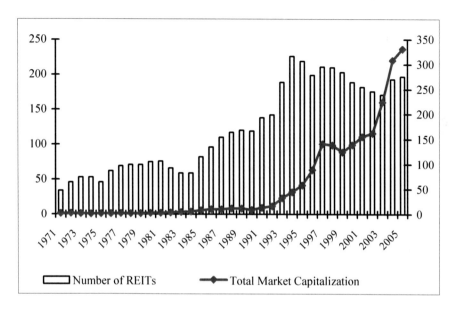

Source: Personal design; data: NAREIT (2006).

As figure IV.1 shows, the steep incline of the total market capitalization line starting in the 1990s resembles the strong growth in market capitalization of the US REIT industry over that time. This growth of the industry also implies a similar growth of the average REIT size. Back in 1992, the average REIT had a market capitalization of $112 million, whereas in 2005, the average REIT had grown to a market capitalization of almost $1.7 billion – resembling a cumulated annual growth rate (CAGR) of more than 23%. This growth in market cap presumably mainly stems from an increase in the average REIT portfolio size. REITs must have been quite active in buying asset portfolios as well as in acquiring other REITs.

IV.2.3 Internationalization of REITs

Since the introduction of REITs in the US in 1960, as outlined above, REIT structures have been introduced and become a widespread asset class in a growing number of countries around the world.[285] The respective national implementations and legal frameworks were thereby generally oriented at the somewhat proven US role model.

In 1969, it was the Netherlands who were the first country to follow the US example when they introduced their local form of a REIT regime. Today, Dutch REITs are amongst the biggest institutional investors in Europe. Probably due to the difficulties in the US REIT industry in the mid-1970s, the REIT concept was still questionable at that time and it took a while until other countries started to adopt the REIT idea. In 1985, Australia – some 16 years later – was the next country to establish a REIT market segment when they introduced "Listed Property Trusts". Today the Australian REIT market is the second largest in the world, second only to the US market..[286] After another five years, the Belgian government reacted to the increasing and uneven competition on the real estate investment market from the neighboring Dutch REITs by introducing its own REIT market segment in 1990.[287]

Table IV.1: Year of Introduction of International REIT Regimes

Country	Year of Introduction
USA	1960
The Netherlands	1969
Australia	1985
Belgium	1990
Canada	1994
Japan	2000
Singapore	2002
Hong Kong	2003
France	2003
UK	2007

Source: ZEW/ebs (2005), p. 2; Drost (2007), p. 21, 24.

As mentioned in the previous section, the US REIT market performed considerably well after the real estate crisis of the ending 1980s and served together with other REIT markets as a positive role model. Interest in the REIT idea started to grow again and the next country to follow was Canada, when it introduced

---

285   For this and the following, cf. ZEW/ebs (2005), p. 1–2.
286   Cf. Tross/Fröhlich (2006), p. 14.
287   For this and the following, cf. ZEW/ebs (2005), p. 1–2.

its own REIT regime in 1994. Six years later Japan established the JREIT in 2000, Singapore adopted the SREIT in 2002 and Hong Kong did the same in 2003. Finally, France also introduced its own REIT regime in 2003. As the interest in REIT structures is still growing internationally, there are many more countries, such as Germany, Malaysia and Taiwan that are seriously considering the introduction of a REIT segment in their respective local markets in the coming years.[288] The UK has introduced its own REIT regime in 2007.[289]

Table IV.1 provides an overview of international REIT regimes.

IV.2.4 Particularities of REITs

As mentioned in section 2.1, due to legal requirements, REITs exhibit characteristics that are different from a "normal" stock company. Most importantly, to retain REIT status they must distribute 80 to 100% of net earnings to their shareholders. These differences also translate into the fact that REITs have a particularly strong desire for growth and at the same time have limited cash accumulation possibilities to finance large acquisition projects needed to fund desired growth, which is illustrated below. This section outlines the special situation of REITs. It thereby concludes the background discussion.

There are two main reasons why REITs have a particularly strong desire for growth: First, due to high payout requirement that create an immediate tax burden at the personal shareholder level, REIT management (in shareholder value terms) is motivated to reduce its shareholders' taxable income today by instead generating future capital gains as a result of future share price increases.[290] If management can deploy an acquisition strategy that increases the real estate portfolio of a REIT and thereby also grows future operating cash flows, then shareholders should be more than compensated for decreased (after-tax) dividends through increases in the share price. This acquisition strategy is particularly suitable if the acquired target has net operating losses that can be effectively utilized by the buyer. Targets of this type are attractive for other REITs, as net operating losses can be carried forward to reduce net income and thereby also lower required payout in the form of dividends.[291] In addition, by buying new assets or other REITs that have new assets, REITs can claim larger depreciation expenses, which directly translate into further reduced dividends and at the same time in-

---

288 Cf. Tross/Fröhlich (2006), p. 14.
289 Cf. Drost (2007), p. 21, 24.
290 For the discussion in this paragraph, cf. Li/Elayan/Meyer (2001), p. 117–118, if not stated differently.
291 Cf. Allen/Sirmans (1987), p. 177.

creases operating cash flow and thereby shareholder value through improved management of the assets.

Second, REITs also have a particularly strong desire for growth, because large REITs are believed to be more efficient than small ones. The main reason for this advantage is seen in REITs being uniquely able to capture various economies of scale.[292] In its most basic form, large REITs are supposed to achieve economies of scale on the expense side as overheads can be spread over a larger asset base.[293] With increasing size, a REIT is also believed to be able to attract higher quality management that has the ability to also generate greater shareholder value.[294] Crocker (1998) even goes one step further when he states that the biggest competitive advantage of Equity Residential (a large REIT in the US) is that, simply due to its size, Equity Residential can attract and invest in high quality management.[295] In addition, larger REITs are believed to achieve economies of scale in marketing as they are usually investing across specific geographic regions.[296]

As a result, REITs should aim for growth as they are especially able to capture economies of scale. In support of this reasoning, Ambrose and Linneman (2001) find that:[297]

- Larger REITs have higher profit margins and rental revenue ratios.
- Larger REITs have lower implied capitalization rates.
- Larger REITs have significantly lower costs of capital. "[...] every billion dollar increase in market capitalization translates into a 2.2% reduction in capital costs".[298]

To conclude, REITs have a strong incentive to go for respectable size as this allows capturing various economies of scale. In addition, acquisitions lead to favorable tax consequences in the short-term.

On the other hand, due to the high pay-out requirements, REITs have special difficulties in generating internal funds to finance large acquisition projects.[299] They can only accumulate funds, if taxable income is less than operating cash flow. Otherwise, depending on the applicable national regulation, the operating cash flow must be (almost) fully distributed to shareholders.[300] In any case, fund

---

292   Cf. Ambrose et al. (2000), p. 212–213.
293   Cf. Linneman (1997), p. 1–12.
294   Cf. Ambrose et al. (2000), p. 212–213.
295   Cf. Crocker (1998), w/p.
296   Cf. Ambrose et al. (2000), p. 212–213.
297   Cf. Ambrose/Linneman (2001), p. 156.
298   Ambrose/Linneman (2001), p. 156.
299   Cf. Campbell/Ghosh/Sirmans (2001), p. 365.
300   Cf. Li/Elayan/Meyer (2001), p. 118.

accumulation possibilities are rather limited due to the institutional structure of REITs. As a consequence, virtually all acquisitions of public targets and most acquisitions of private targets in the REIT industry are being financed solely with stock.[301]

To conclude, resulting from their institutional structure and operating characteristics, REITs have considerable incentives to pursue growth strategies. Through the implementation of effective growth and/or acquisition strategies, REITs can substantially optimize the after-tax return of their shareholders and thereby increase shareholder value. Moreover, realized growth strategies allow the grown REITs to enjoy the benefits of captured economies of scale. In addition, the analysis in section IV.2.2 has already shown that the observed market development of the past 15 years, with the average REIT having significantly grown in size, resembles this line of argument.

IV.3 Literature Review and Hypotheses Generation

IV.3.1 Literature Review

Evidence on wealth effects of REIT M&A is rather limited in comparison to the large amount of empirical studies that have dealt with acquisitions in the related international banking industry.[302] However, there is some prior research on M&A of REITs. These studies all utilize event study methodology and analyze the shareholder value effects of transaction announcements of REIT acquisitions. To the best of the author's knowledge, only six prior studies deal with effects of REIT M&A. The results are summarized in the following paragraphs.[303]

The first study on REIT M&A was undertaken by Allen and Sirmans in 1987.[304] They examined wealth effects to the bidders' shareholders from the announcement of 38 completed transactions between 1977 and 1983, where both buyer and target were a REIT. Allen and Sirmans found a significant wealth increase for acquiring shareholders. They assume the primary source of this value gain to be improved management of the acquired assets. Leading to this conclu-

---

301 Cf. Campbell/Ghosh/Sirmans (2001), p. 361.
302 Cf. Kirchhoff/Schiereck/Mentz (2006), w/p, and Li/Elayan/Meyer (2001), p. 115.
303 Research on REIT portfolio and asset acquisitions is explicitly not included here, as it is a different strand of research and does not allow a meaningful comparison with the M&A literature. For an overview cf. e.g. Campbell/Petrova/Sirmans (2003), p. 347–366, McIntosh/Ott/Liang (1995), p. 299–307, and Elayan/Young (1994), p. 167–182.
304 Cf. Allen/Sirmans (1987), p. 175–184.

sion was the fact that mergers between two REITs of the same type (mortgage or equity) exhibited a significantly larger wealth effect when compared to mergers of different types.

McIntosh, Officer and Born (1989) capitalized on the work of Allen and Sirmans (1987) when they analyzed the impact of acquisitions on target shareholder wealth (where the target was a REIT).[305] Their sample includes 27 transactions between July, 1962 and December, 1986. Results indicated an abnormal drift prior to the announcement that was not significant. At the announcement event, however, a small positive and significant wealth effect for the target shareholders was found.

Campbell, Ghosh and Sirmans (1998) analyze a sample of 27 completed mergers of publicly traded equity REITs which occurred between 1994 and January 1998.[306] They calculate three- and five-day abnormal returns for both bidder and target REITs. In their sample, shareholders of acquiring REITs lose 1.5% and shareholders of target REITs gain 5.2%, on average, over the five-day event window. Unfortunately, they do not report the statistical significance of their results.

In their second study, Campbell, Ghosh and Sirmans (2001) focus on the information content of the method of payment in REIT mergers.[307] Their sample includes a larger sample of 85 transactions between the beginning of 1994 and the end of 1998 in which the bidder is a publicly traded equity REIT. On the target side, only 40 REITs are listed with the remaining 45 targets being privately held. Interestingly, their results show that acquirers of privately held targets exhibit a positive abnormal return of 1.9%, on average, over the three day window, whereas acquirers of publicly traded targets experience a negative abnormal return of 0.6%.[308] On the other hand, shareholders of publicly traded targets enjoy a 3.2% positive abnormal return over the same interval, which is consistent with McIntosh, Officer and Born (1989), but again is much smaller than for targets in non-REIT mergers.[309] The mentioned results are all significant at the 10%-level. Another interesting finding of their study is that acquiring shareholders' wealth effects are negatively related to the acquirer's size, which the authors attribute to larger REITs being inclined to overpay.[310]

---

305 Cf. McIntosh/Officer/Born (1989), p. 141–155.
306 Cf. Campbell/Ghosh/Sirmans (1998), p. 45–54.
307 Cf. Campbell/Ghosh/Sirmans (2001), p. 361–387.
308 This finding is consistent with blockholder theory. Cf. Shleifer/Vishny (1986), p. 461–488.
309 Cf. Campbell/Ghosh/Sirmans (2001), p. 373.
310 Cf. Campbell/Ghosh/Sirmans (2001), p. 379.

As part of a broader study, Young and Elayan (2002) analyze 24 mergers between REITs that occurred from 1972 to 1991.[311] In their sample, the bidders' shareholders experienced unexpected wealth effects of 0.84% and the targets' shareholders effects of 0.97%, respectively. It is surprising, however, why they chose such an old data set in 2002 and, moreover, also find less transactions in a longer and overlapping period as compared to Allen/Sirmans (1987).

The latest literature on wealth effects of REIT M&A is a study conducted by Sahin (2005).[312] The study focuses on a sample containing 35 acquisitions between REITs from 1994 to 1998 and analyzes both short- and long-term performance. Short-term results indicate that bidders experience statistically significant negative wealth effects of 1.2%, whereas target shareholders earn statistically significant positive abnormal returns of 4.3% in a three-day interval around the announcement day.

Table IV.2 provides an overview of the prior research studies that have been presented above.

Table IV.2: Prior Research on Wealth Effects in REIT M&A

Paper	Data	Time Period	Summary of Results
Allen/Sirmans (1987)	Bidders in 38 M&A	1977–1983	Bidders experience significant positive wealth effects.
McIntosh/Officer/Born (1989)	Targets in 27 M&A	1962–1986	Targets experience significant positive wealth effects.
Campbell/Ghosh/Sirmans (1998)	Targets and bidders in 27 M&A	1994–1998	Bidders experience negative and targets experience positive wealth effects. Statistical significance is not reported.
Campbell/Ghosh/Sirmans (2001)	85 bidders and 40 targets in 85 M&A	1994–1998	Bidders experience small negative wealth effects, if target is public, and positive wealth effects, if target is private. Public targets experience positive wealth effects. All effects are statistically significant.
Young/Elayan (2002)	Targets and bidders in 24 M&A	1972–1991	Bidders and targets both experience small positive wealth effects.
Sahin (2005)	Targets and bidders in 35 M&A	1994–1998	Bidders experience small negative wealth effects, while targets experience positive wealth effects. Both effects are statistically significant.

Source: Personal summary in the style of Zietz/Sirmans/Friday (2003), p. 129–134.

---

311 Cf. Young/Elayan (2002), p. 27–32.
312 Cf. Sahin (2005), p. 321–342.

To conclude, prior research on wealth effects of REIT M&A is not only limited with regard to the mere number of studies. Even less convincing are the shortcomings with regard to sample size as well as to the periods covered. Other than Campbell/Ghosh/Sirmans (2001), all other studies suffer from small sample sizes that range from between 24 to 38 transactions. Such limited amount of data is generally not sufficient to draw meaningful general conclusions on the REIT industry as a whole.[313] In addition, there is no existing study which includes REIT transactions after the year 1998. Three of the six studies do not even contain any data from the modern REIT era after 1992/1993, which is different in many aspects from the industry of prior years.[314] Finally, all studies have a distinct US focus. There is no research on the modern international REIT industry that covers all international transactions until present. This paper aims to fill the identified research gaps.

IV.3.2 Hypotheses Generation

As long as REIT managers are acting in the best interest of their shareholders, both target and bidder shareholders should get value from an M&A transaction, as only in this case would management undertake the merger. Under the assumption that market participants can realistically gauge the influence of the transaction at announcement, the value increase should resemble both synergy potential and takeover premium as well as negotiation skills of both sides. However, specific research on REITs provides a different view. Most cross-sectional studies and especially those for the related banking industry find mixed or rather small negative abnormal returns for the bidders as well as for bidder sub-samples.[315] Prior research on REIT M&A, which was presented in the last section, yields similar results. It seems that the considerable benefits REITs gain from growing in size, which was reported by Ambrose/Limmeman (2001),[316] are being more than compensated by other factors. These arguments lead to hypothesis 1a.

Hypothesis 1a)   The announcement has an abnormal negative effect on bidder share price.

---

313 To be considered a sufficient size, a sample should include at least 50 transactions.
      Cf. Brown/Warner (1985), p. 5.
314 Cf. e.g. Ambrose/Linneman (2001), p. 141–162 for arguments on the modern REIT
      era, which mainly is a result of the amendments made by the TRA in 1986.
315 Cf. e.g. Chang (1998), p. 773–784, Pilloff (1996), p. 294–310, and Travlos (1987),
      p. 943–963.
316 Cf. Ambrose/Linneman (2001), p. 156.

Prior evidence on target shareholder abnormal returns is clearer cut. Broad event studies find large positive wealth effects for the target shareholders even in the range of 12% to 22%.[317] However, prior research on REIT M&A suggests a positive, but rather moderate expectation on abnormal target returns when compared to the broader studies.[318] Figures range from almost one percent to five; the study of Campbell/Ghosh/Sirmans (2001) finds an abnormal return of 3.2% for the group of targets. Accordingly, the announcement is expected to have a small, but significant abnormal wealth effect for target shareholders.

Hypothesis 1b)   The announcement has an abnormal positive effect on target share price.

In assessing M&A announcement effects, an important distinction can be made between public-to-public and public-to-private mergers. If a transaction is financed with stock,[319] private target firm owners often gain a large ownership position in the combined entity. According to monitoring theory, these blockholders can favorably influence the development of the company/stock.[320] In addition, the willingness of the new blockholders to hold such large positions provides a positive signal to the market. Campbell, Ghosh and Sirmans (2001) built two sub-samples to address this question and found significant differences between the two.[321] As mentioned in the literature review, acquirers of privately held targets exhibited a positive abnormal return of 1.9%, on average, over the three day window, whereas acquirers of publicly traded targets experienced a negative abnormal return of 0.6%. Faccio, McConnell and Stolin (2006) come to similar findings, but conclude that "[...] fundamental factors that give rise to this listing effect [...] remain elusive".[322] In any case, a more positive abnormal return for acquirers of private targets could be found and the resulting hypothesis 2 is based on these previous findings.

Hypothesis 2)   Acquirers of private targets experience more positive wealth effects when compared to acquirers of public targets.

As all previous studies on REIT M&A had a distinct US focus, the question remains whether there is a difference in returns that are dependent on the geo-

---

317   Cf. e.g. Huang/Walkling (1987), p. 329–349, and Jensen/Ruback (1983), p. 5–50.
318   Cf. Campbell/Ghosh/Sirmans (2001), p. 373.
319   This is the case in almost all REIT transactions. Cf. Campbell/Ghosh/Sirmans (2001), p. 361.
320   Cf. Shleifer/Vishny (1986), p. 461–488.
321   Cf. Campbell/Ghosh/Sirmans (2001), p. 361–387.
322   Faccio/McConnell/Stolin (2006), p. 197.

graphic market. Surely, one key addition of the present study is its broader, international research focus. Therefore, two sub-samples are built in order to find differences in returns of US- vs. non-US transactions. However, there is no indication of what the direction or the magnitude of this influence might be.

Hypothesis 3)   US- vs. non-US transactions lead to different abnormal returns for both bidder and target.

Value expectations on M&A transactions can also systematically change with general market sentiment over time. Shleifer and Vishny (2003) find this relationship in their study and explain takeover waves with an irrational market and self-oriented managers.[323] Rhodes-Kropf and Viswanathan (2007) also provide evidence on the relationship between takeover waves and general overvaluation.[324] Concurrent with this school of thought and as there are no prior studies which covered the period after 1998, I will assess if there are any significant differences due to market sentiment in the first and second half of the sample period.[325]

Hypothesis 4)   Due to market sentiment, abnormal returns change over time. As a result, value effects are different in period one from period two.

Table IV.3 provides an overview of the proposed hypotheses.

Table IV.3: Overview of Hypotheses

1a	The announcement has an abnormal negative effect on bidder share price.
1b	The announcement has an abnormal positive effect on target share price.
2	Acquirers of private targets experience more positive wealth effects compared to acquirers of public targets.
3	US- vs. non-US transactions lead to different abnormal returns for both bidder and target.
4	Due to market sentiment abnormal returns change over time. As a result, value effects are different in period one from period two.

Source: Personal design.

---

323   Cf. Shleifer/Vishny (2003), p. 295–311.
324   Cf. Rhodes-Kropf/Viswanathan (2007), w/p.
325   As the first transaction took place in 1993, the 13 years from 1993 to 2005 are divided into two 6.5 year periods (period one from 01/01/1993 to 06/30/1999 and period two from 07/01/1999 to 12/31/2005).

IV.4 Event Study Analysis

IV.4.1 Applied Methodology

IV.4.1.1 Market Model and Abnormal Returns

This study employs event study methodology to assess whether there are any abnormal value effects as a result of M&A announcements in the REIT industry. Event study methodology has been applied in a large body of scientific research[326] as it yields a reliable measure of the value created through an M&A announcement; i.e. the event study approach is suitable to our research question. This study assesses the abnormal effects of acquisition announcements on both bidder and target shareholder value. As markets are assumed to be informational efficient[327], the announcement of the M&A transaction will disseminate quickly in the marketplace.[328] If arrival of this new information then changes the market view about bidder and/or target involved in the announced transaction, then their prices should correctly reflect this restatement of expectations. As a result, abnormal returns can usually be exhibited around the announcement.

Because of the widespread application of event studies, there are numerous different methods for the individual steps. Peterson (1989) already stated that there is no such thing as a standard event study methodology.[329] Accordingly, the following describes the methodology chosen for our study.

Most importantly, the market model put forward by Dodd/Warner (1983) and Brown/Warner (1985)[330] to calculate expected returns R_{jt} for stock j at time t is applied:

$$(1) \quad R_{jt} = \alpha_j + \beta_j R_{mt} + \varepsilon_{jt}$$

Where: R_{jt} return of stock j on day t
                R_{mt} market return on day t

α_j intercept
β_j coefficient
ε_{jt} error term

---

326 Cf. Khotari/Warner (2004), p. 4.
327 In the semi-strong form.
328 Cf. Fama (1970), p. 383–417, and Fama (1976), p. 143–145, on the idea of information efficiency.
329 Cf. Peterson (1989), p. 36.
330 Cf. Dodd/Warner (1983), p. 401–438, and Brown/Warner (1985), p. 3–31.

Ordinary least squares (OLS)-regressions for each individual stock are used over the estimation period, with stocks being the dependent and the respective market indices the explaining variable in order to calculate regression intercept α_j and coefficient β_j. Intercept and coefficient are then used to calculate expected returns from the observed market returns in the event window:

(2) $E(R_{jt}) = \alpha_j + \beta_j R_{mt}$

Where: $E(R_{jt})$ expected return of stock j on day t

This expected return is then subtracted from the observed stock return, which yields the abnormal return AR_{jt} of stock j on day t.

(3) $AR_{jt} = R_{jt} - E(R_{jt})$

In the next step, abnormal returns are aggregated (summed up) over the event window(s) to give the cumulated abnormal return $CAR_{j\,[t1;t2]}$ for each of n stocks in the sample.

(4) $CAR_{j[t_1;t_2]} = \sum_{t_1}^{t_2} AR_{jt}$

Finally, the CARs are aggregated over the stocks and divided by n to yield the cumulated average abnormal return $CAAR_{[t1;t2]}$ of the group.

(5) $CAAR_{[t_1;t_2]} = \frac{1}{n} \cdot \sum_{j}^{n} CAR_{j[t_1;t_2]}$

Test statistics then determine the statistical significance of the observed CAARs. I apply the Boehmer-Test[331], as this is the only test statistic which explicitly accounts for a possible variance increase during the event period and thereby leads to more robust results than other test statistics.[332] In addition, I use mean difference tests to check for significance of differences between the sub-sample CAARs.

---

331   Cf. Boehmer/Musumeci/Poulsen (1991), p. 253–272.
332   Cf. Sera (2002), p. 6.

IV.4.1.2 Event Window Selection

The event window should be long enough so that all share price reactions related to the transaction announcement can be captured. On the other hand, the event window should be kept short enough in order not to include any confounding effects.[333] Within this study, an event window T of 41 days is considered: T = [–20;20], where t = {0} denominates the announcement date of a transaction. For example, the returns of 20 trading days prior to 20 days after the announcement are analyzed. In addition, I also calculate the CAARs for the following six sub event windows: [–20;0], [–5;0], {0}, [–1;1], [0;5], [0;20].

To estimate the model parameters needed in the expected return calculations, an estimation period of between 100 to 300 days can be chosen.[334] Campbell, Gosh and Sirmans (2001) apply a rather short 108 day estimation period "[...] considering the environment of rapid change that prevailed among REITs in the 1990s."[335] This study takes a more conservative approach by applying a 160 day estimation period that should provide more solid regression results.

Figure IV.2 below illustrates the estimation period and event window selection.

Figure IV.2: Estimation Period and Event Window Selection

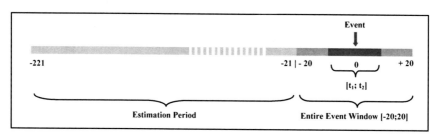

Source: Personal design concurrent with e.g. Peterson (1989), p. 38.

IV.4.2 Sample and Data Selection

Samples should be of sufficient size to provide meaningful results. For this reason, a very long sample period has been chosen that encompasses the whole

---

333   Cf. McWilliams/Siegel (1997), p. 636.
334   Cf. Peterson (1989), p. 38.
335   Campbell/Ghosh/Sirmans (2001), p. 371.

modern REIT era from the beginning of the 1990s until present. In addition, for the first time in REIT research, this study includes international data in the data sample by covering all global REIT markets. To identify relevant REIT M&A transactions, Thomson Financial SDC (Securities Data Company – M&A Database) was used as the prime data source. Individual stock and index return data for both bidder and targets were provided by Datastream, which is also from Thomson Financial. Relevant transactions were identified and selected according to the following criteria:

- The transaction was announced between January 1, 1990 and December 31, 2005.
- All transactions globally, where target and bidder was a REIT.[336]
- Transaction volume exceeded $100 million.
- Target or bidder were exchange listed at announcement.
- A change of corporate control has occurred during the transaction (>50% only after transaction).
- Deal status is completed.

This request yielded a deal list of 183 transactions. Unfortunately, the list included transactions with real estate investment firms, which where wrongfully also identified as REITs. However, all of these non-REITs could clearly be identified through company research on factiva and the internet. If a non-REIT was on at least one side of the transaction, the deal was taken off the list. As a result, the list of pure REIT M&A shortened to 116 transactions. Finally, nine more deals needed to be deleted as some transactions had a private REIT on both sides and as some stocks didn't show enough liquidity, i.e. price movements. The final list consists of 107 M&A transactions where, at announcement, both bidder and target were a REIT and where at least one side was publicly listed (over the estimation period and event window).

IV.4.3 Descriptive Statistics

Within our sample of 107 M&A transactions, 93 bidders and 79 targets were publicly listed and had sufficient trading on the market. As a result, a total of 172 REITs entered the event study calculations. This first of all provides a broad and solid data basis to gain meaningful results on REIT M&A. To test the hypotheses, several sub-samples for both bidders and targets were constructed. Table

---

336 I.e. included are those deals where both parties are described as a REIT in their respective business descriptions in the database.

IV.4 provides an overview of the formed sub-samples and of the number of REITs included in each of them.

Table IV.4: Sample and Sub-sample Overview

Total Number of REIT Transactions incl. in Sample			107
Total Number of Bidders	93	**Total Number of Targets**	79
Bidder Subsamples		*Target Subsamples*	
Private Target	23	Private Target	NA
Public Target	70	Public Target	NA
US-Deal	73	US-Deal	60
Non-US Deal	20	Non-US Deal	19
First Period	48	First Period	37
Second Period	45	Second Period	42

Source: Personal design; data: Thomson SDC.

Public-to-public mergers have dominated REIT consolidation; there are only 23 bidders which acquired private REITs. The remaining 70 bidders aimed at public targets. As expected from the sheer dominance of the American market in terms of size and maturity, most transactions occurred in the US. 85 of the 107 transactions in the sample had a distinct US focus. In contrast to other event studies that focus on different industries, it is interesting to note that there is not a single cross border transaction in the data set. All REIT M&A took place within national borders. The inexistence of cross-border acquisitions is considered as an indicator of divergence in national institutional settings, which might induce high integration costs for cross-border transactions. Besides those 85 M&A that occurred in the US, the remaining transactions took place in Australia (the second largest REIT market globally) as well as in Canada. The other markets are probably still too young and/or too small to consolidate via REIT M&A activity.

With regard to M&A occurrence over time, the transactions are almost equally split over the two analyzed periods. However, the individual years have been quite heterogeneous. After the real estate crisis, consolidation activity picked up slowly in 1993/1994 and then quickly rose to its peak in 1997/1998 with 16 and 15 transactions, respectively. After that, the M&A market for REITs gradually declined until 2002 before it rose again strongly in 2003 and 2004. The last year has been rather quiet with regard to REIT M&A. Figure IV.3 shows the number of REIT transactions which are included in the data sample, by year.

Figure IV.3: REIT Transactions included in Data Sample over Time

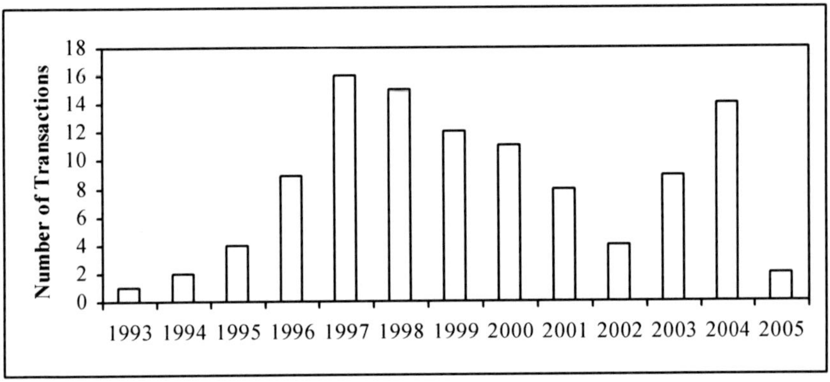

Source: Personal design; data: Thomson SDC.

Within the transaction sample, acquiring REITs are, on average ,about three times as large as target REITs.[337] The average (mean) market capitalizations a-mount to $1.570 billion for the group of bidders and $559 million for the group of targets. The mean transaction rank value is larger, of course, than the average target and amounts to $1.027 billion. This implies that common equity makes up about 54% of the average target REIT capital structure.

IV.4.4 Event Study Results

IV.4.4.1 Bidders and Targets

In the aggregate, I find a total value destruction of $1.776 billion for the bidders and a value generation of $3.368 billion for the targets caused by the 107 M&A announcements in the transaction sample over the three-day interval surrounding the announcement [-1;1].[338] Overall, REIT M&A thus create value for the com-bined entity amounting to an overall aggregate value of $ 1.591 billion. The ob-served value creation for the group of targets is almost twice as large as the value loss for the bidders. When calculating the combined entity view with average value generation/destruction figures of all transactions in the sample, I find an

---

337 Please note that these figures are biased, as only listed entities are reflected.
338 Again, these figures are biased as only listed entities are reflected.

average value generation of $23.5 million per acquisition or $2.518 billion in the aggregate for the combined entity. REIT M&A have thus clearly created value for the combined entity (in the event window [–1;1]).

Figure IV.4 illustrates the cumulated average abnormal return (CAAR) development of both bidders and targets over the entire event window.

Figure IV.4: CAAR Development over the entire Event Window

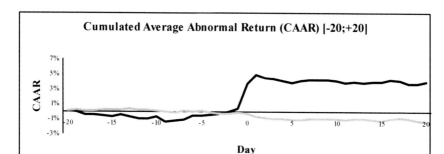

Source: Personal calculations; data: Datastream.

As figure IV.4 shows, bidders experience a small negative revaluation of their shares after the announcement, whereas targets exhibit a considerable value gain beginning at the announcement day. As expected by market efficiency requirements, the largest part of the announcement effects can be observed at announcement, when the new information reaches the market. Here, the CAAR of the targets jumps considerably by about 5% and stabilizes afterwards.

Table IV.5 provides a more comprehensive view for both bidders and targets as it illustrates the exact CAARs for the seven event windows as well as the test statistics.

Table IV.5 shows that bidders, on average, experience virtually no abnormal return at announcement and small negative returns in all other event windows. Over the entire event window [–20;20], a negative return of –1.35% is found, which is highly significant at the 1%-level. The slightly smaller negative returns in the event windows [0;5] and [0;20] are still significant at the 5% level. Overall results rather point towards a negative assessment of the transactions for bidder shareholders. Concerning the group of acquired targets, abnormal value effects are clearer cut. Target CAARs are clearly positive and highly significant at the

1%-level in all seven event windows. They vary between 3.39% and a maximum of 4.95% for the event windows {0} and [–1;1], respectively. Significant value has thus been created for the target shareholders in the amount of three to five percent depending on the individual event window.

Table IV.5: CAARs of all Bidders and Targets

	Bidders				Targets		
N=93	CAAR	P-Value	Sig.	N=79	CAAR	P-Value	Sig.
[–20;20]	–1.35%	0.0091	***	[–20;20]	3.90%	0.0008	***
[–20;0]	–0.32%	0.1861		[–20;0]	3.67%	0.0001	***
[–5;0]	–0.31%	0.2226		[–5;0]	4.32%	0.0000	***
{0}	–0.07%	0.7624		{0}	3.39%	0.0000	***
[–1;1]	–0.41%	0.1595		[–1;1]	4.95%	0.0000	***
[0;5]	–0.89%	0.0256	**	[0;5]	3.48%	0.0002	***
[0;20]	–1.10%	0.0135	**	[0;20]	3.62%	0.0005	***

Note: ***=significant at 1%-level; **=significant at 5%-level; *=significant at 10%-level.
Source: Personal calculations; data: Datastream.

IV.4.4.2 Announcement Effects according to Target Status

To find out whether target status has an effect on bidder returns, bidders were divided into two sub-groups: Bidders that acquired private- and bidders that acquired public targets. As expected, the two groups experience quite different CAARs, which are displayed in detail in table IV.6 below.

Table IV.6: Bidder CAARs in Acquisitions of Private vs. Public Targets

Bidders – Priv. Target				Bidders – Pub. Target				Meandifference		
N=23	CAAR	P-Value	Sig.	N=70	CAAR	P-Value	Sig.	CAAR	P-Value	Sig.
[–20;20]	1.60%	0.3789		[–20;20]	–2.32%	0.0006	***	3.92%	0.0356	**
[–20;0]	1.62%	0.2095		[–20;0]	–0.96%	0.0218	**	2.59%	0.1162	
[–5;0]	0.44%	0.7112		[–5;0]	–0.55%	0.1132		0.99%	0.2663	
[0]	0.45%	0.3059		[0]	–0.24%	0.5215		0.69%	0.1920	
[–1;1]	0.66%	0.5384		[–1;1]	–0.76%	0.0606	*	1.42%	0.0819	*
[0;5]	–0.01%	0.9259		[0;5]	–1.18%	0.0147	**	1.17%	0.2311	
[0;20]	0.43%	0.7677		[0;20]	–1.60%	0.0045	***	2.02%	0.0524	*

Note: ***=significant at 1%-level; **=significant at 5%-level; *=significant at 10%-level.
Source: Personal calculations; data: Datastream.

As expected, CAARs of bidders acquiring private targets are almost all positive, particularly in the days prior to the announcement. They vary between –0.01% and 1.62% in the event windows [0;5] and [–20;0], respectively. However, the returns of this group are not significant in the Boehmer test (probably due to the small number of observations in this group amounting to 23). In contrast to this group, those bidders that acquire public targets exhibit negative abnormal returns, which are also larger compared to the group of all bidders. CAARs range from –0.24% on the announcement day to –2.32% over the entire event window and are significant for five out of seven event windows. Differences for the groups are considerable and partly significant. Over the entire event window, the CAAR difference amounts to 3.92% and is significant at the 5%-level, implying significant differences between the two sub-samples.

IV.4.4.3 Announcement Effects according to Country

Announcement effects in the REIT industry also vary to some extent depending on the country where the transaction took place. As most acquisitions were undertaken in the US, bidder and target groups were subdivided into US- and non-US deals. Table IV.7 illustrates findings with respect to this grouping of sub-samples below.

Table IV.7: CAARS of US Bidders vs. Non-US Bidders

	Bidders – US			Bidders – Non-US			Meandifference		
N=73	CAAR	P-Value	Sig.	N=20	CAAR	P-Value	Sig.	CAAR	P-Value	Sig.
[–20;20]	–1.27%	0.0224	**	[–20;20]	–1.64%	0.2100		0.37%	0.8236	
[–20;0]	–0.65%	0.0619	*	[–20;0]	0.86%	0.3789		–1.51%	0.2706	
[–5;0]	–0.66%	0.0383	**	[–5;0]	0.98%	0.0425	**	–1.64%	0.0116	**
[0]	–0.28%	0.3137		[0]	0.69%	0.1031		–0.97%	0.0854	*
[–1;1]	–0.61%	0.0765	*	[–1;1]	0.32%	0.6293		–0.93%	0.2736	
[0;5]	–1.17%	0.0103	**	[0;5]	0.16%	0.7525		–1.33%	0.1518	
[0;20]	–0.90%	0.0579	*	[0;20]	–1.81%	0.1010		0.92%	0.4395	

Note: ***=significant at 1%-level; **=significant at 5%-level; *=significant at 10%-level.
Source: Personal calculations; data: Datastream.

As table IV.7 shows, bidders in the US experience small negative returns in all event windows, of which returns in six event windows are significant. Bidders in non-US deals exhibit slightly larger negative returns over the entire event window, but the remaining CAARs are almost all positive. Only the 0.98% abnormal return in the [–5;0] window is significant (at the 5%-level), however. The mean difference test shows (only in this event window and at announcement) that the CAARs of the two groups are significantly different from one another, implying some significance in the differences of returns. Results and their weak significance are again also driven by the limited number of observations on non-US bidders.

Table IV.8 below illustrates the CAARs of the two target groups according to the geographic location. Again, results for the targets are generally more significant as compared to the bidders and are all positive. Over the entire event window, US-targets gain more than non-US targets with 4.34% as compared to 2.49%, on average . However, the differences are only significant in the three-day interval around the announcement (10%-level) and over the [0;20] event window (5%-level). This is again partly driven by the limited number of observations of non-US targets. Results indicate, however, that CAARs tend to be about two times larger for target shareholders in US REIT transactions as compared to non-US transactions.

Table IV.8: CAARs of US Targets vs. Non-US Targets

	Targets – US				Targets – Non-US			Meandifference		
N=60	CAAR	P-Value	Sig.	N=19	CAAR	P-Value	Sig.	CAAR	P-Value	Sig.
[–20;20]	4.34%	0.0045	***	[–20;20]	2.49%	0.0108	**	1.85%	0.3211	
[–20;0]	3.43%	0.0040	***	[–20;0]	4.42%	0.0014	***	–0.99%	0.5661	
[–5;0]	4.56%	0.0001	***	[–5;0]	3.55%	0.0002	***	1.01%	0.4562	
[0]	3.56%	0.0005	***	[0]	2.84%	0.0035	***	0.73%	0.5830	
[–1;1]	5.62%	0.0000	***	[–1;1]	2.86%	0.0295	**	2.76%	0.0848	*
[0;5]	4.00%	0.0008	***	[0;5]	1.85%	0.1056		2.15%	0.1904	
[0;20]	4.48%	0.0005	***	[0;20]	0.92%	0.4498		3.56%	0.0364	**

Note: ***=significant at 1%-level; **=significant at 5%-level; *=significant at 10%-level.
Source: Personal calculations; data: Datastream.

IV.4.4.4 Announcement Effects over Time

Announcement effects can also systematically vary over time. As the second focus of the study is an extension over time to cover even the latest transactions, the covered period is subdivided into two equal halves. The first period includes transactions from 1993 to the middle of 1999 and the second period includes those deals which were announced in the second half of 1999 to 2005. Again, this results in two sub-samples for bidders as well as for targets. As table IV.9 illustrates, there are some differences between bidder returns in the first and the second period.

Table IV.9: CAARs of Bidders in the First vs. Second Period

	Bidders – First Per.				Bidders – Second Per.			Meandifference		
N=48	CAAR	P-Value	Sig.	N=45	CAAR	P-Value	Sig.	CAAR	P-Value	Sig.
[–20;20]	0.31%	0.4098		[–20;20]	–3.12%	0.0056	***	3.42%	0.0412	**
[–20;0]	0.63%	0.7171		[–20;0]	–1.34%	0.1310		1.97%	0.1689	
[–5;0]	–0.02%	0.5189		[–5;0]	–0.61%	0.2827		0.59%	0.4112	
[0]	0.03%	0.7681		[0]	–0.17%	0.8832		0.19%	0.7355	
[–1;1]	–0.08%	0.3797		[–1;1]	–0.76%	0.2749		0.69%	0.3925	
[0;5]	–0.62%	0.0854	*	[0;5]	–1.18%	0.1495		0.56%	0.5536	
[0;20]	–0.30%	0.4254		[0;20]	–1.95%	0.0076	***	1.65%	0.1014	

Note: ***=significant at 1%-level; **=significant at 5%-level; *=significant at 10%-level.

Source: Personal calculations; data: Datastream.

While returns of bidders in the first period are rather positive up to the announcement, they are slightly negative in the event windows after the announcement. However, almost all CAARs are insignificant. Bidders in the second period exhibit abnormal returns which are all negative and larger in magnitude. Over the entire event window [–20;20], the CAAR amounts to –3.12%, which is significant at the 1%-level, and is almost 3.5% less than the 0.31% of the first period bidders. This is also the only event window which shows significant differences in the observed CAARs (5%-level).

Table IV.10: CAARs of Targets in the First vs. Second Period

	Targets – First Per.				Targets – Second Per.			Meandifference		
N=37	CAAR	P-Value	Sig.	N=42	CAAR	P-Value	Sig.	CAAR	P-Value	Sig.
[–20;20]	3.08%	0.0433	**	[–20;20]	4.62%	0.0082	***	–1.53%	0.5197	
[–20;0]	2.10%	0.0568	*	[–20;0]	5.05%	0.0007	***	–2.95%	0.1130	
[–5;0]	3.45%	0.0002	***	[–5;0]	5.08%	0.0004	***	–1.63%	0.3069	
[0]	2.09%	0.0045	***	[0]	4.54%	0.0008	***	–2.45%	0.0941	*
[–1;1]	3.89%	0.0004	***	[–1;1]	5.89%	0.0001	***	–2.00%	0.2560	
[0;5]	1.97%	0.0694	*	[0;5]	4.81%	0.0011	***	–2.84%	0.1183	
[0;20]	3.07%	0.0085	***	[0;20]	4.11%	0.0167	**	–1.04%	0.5959	

Note: ***=significant at 1%-level; **=significant at 5%-level; *=significant at 10%-level.

Source: Personal calculations; data: Datastream.

Table IV.10 displays the results for the two target sub-samples. It shows that there are apparent differences in relation to market sentiment between the two groups. Although CAARs are positive for both over all event windows, abnormal returns are considerably larger in the second period than those of the first period. CAARs in the second period are almost twice as large. Consequently, significance levels of abnormal returns are also generally higher in the second period. Considering the results of the mean difference tests, however, only the 2.45% difference at the announcement day is significant (at the 10%-level). For example, there is only weak evidence that CAARs differ significantly in the first and the second period.

IV.4.5 Discussion

As expected, small negative returns for the group of bidders are found. Only the CAARs of the event windows [–20;20], [0;5] and [0;20] are significant, and the results seem to confirm hypothesis 1a, i.e. that the considerable benefits acquiring REITs gain from size are indeed more than compensated for by other factors. For the shareholders of acquiring REITs, M&A transactions do not generate value but instead rather destroy some value. In contrast, the abnormal returns within the group of targets are clearly positive and highly significant, which confirms hypothesis 1b. As the CAARS are positive and highly significant in all event windows, there is considerable value created for the target shareholders through the transactions, which is a little larger when compared to the findings of previous studies.

This positive wealth effect could, however, also be interrelated with the small negative bidder returns, implying that bidders simply paid too much for the transactions. Accordingly, value would have been transferred from bidder to target shareholders. But importantly, as mentioned above, the value increase for the targets is larger in absolute terms than the value destruction for the bidders. Implying a positive overall wealth effect for the combined entity REIT M&A can therefore be considered as value creating in the aggregate. There are some synergies involved in REIT M&A that the market seems to acknowledge, which the make the combined entity worth more than the individual REITs . However, bidders seem to have overpaid and thereby passed over more than the anticipated benefits from the transaction to the target shareholders.

Expectations on the effect of target status on bidder returns are also supported by the results. There are significant differences in CAARs of bidders depending on the status of the target. Bidders acquiring public targets exhibit more negative returns compared to the group of all bidders and acquirers of private targets conversely enjoy small positive returns. These differences are quite similar to those found by Campbell, Ghosh and Sirmans (2001).[339] Obviously, the willingness of new blockholders to hold large positions in the new entity and their ability to better monitor management provides a positive signal to the market. Another possible explanation might be that private targets can be bought for lower prices, on average, as they do not have an observable market price.

As all previous studies on REIT M&A had a distinct US-focus, the question remained whether there is a difference in returns depending on the geographic region. The results for both bidder and target groups show some differences in CAARs. Whilst the returns for the US-bidders are strictly small and negative, the returns for the non-US bidders are somewhat mixed. No clear relationship can be established here, although differences are significant in two sub-windows. It is quite similar with the target groups. Here it seems that targets in US transactions exhibited larger wealth effects than targets in non-US transactions. However, the differences again are only significant in two sub-windows.

Value effects of M&A transactions can systematically change over time. For the REIT industry, this seems to be applicable as well. Interestingly, changing market sentiment appears to have had opposite effects on bidders and targets in the REIT industry. On one side, bidders experience larger and more significant negative returns in the second period, whereas in the first period, returns were close to zero and rather insignificant. On the other side, targets in the first period gain less than those acquired in the second period, which gain more and in which CAARs are more significant. It appears as if market sentiment or maybe other factors had the opposite effect on targets and bidders. This could be an indication of increased competition in the acquisition of targets in the second period, which led to more severe overpaying. In any case, it is an indicator for a rising wealth transfer over time. While bidder stocks show increasing negative abnormal returns in the announcement window over time, the target owners' CAARs become increasingly positive. In light of this evidence, market sentiment seems to have a considerable impact on shareholder wealth effects. Hypothesis 4 is confirmed in that sense.

Table IV.11 summarizes the results with respect to the proposed hypotheses.

---

339 Cf. Campbell/Ghosh/Sirmans (2001), p. 361–387.

Table IV.11: Overview of Hypotheses Confirmation

1a	The announcement has an abnormal negative effect on bidder share price.	confirmed
1b	The announcement has an abnormal positive effect on target share price.	confirmed
2	Acquirers of private targets experience more positive wealth effects compared to acquirers of public targets.	confirmed
3	US- vs. non-US transactions lead to different abnormal returns for both bidder and target.	weakly confirmed
4	Due to market sentiment abnormal returns change over time. As a result, value effects are different in period one from period two.	confirmed

Source: Personal design.

IV.5 Conclusion

Despite the long history of REITs, the growing number of REIT regimes and the large amount of capital REITs represent, prior research on M&A between REITs has been rather limited. This is even more surprising as since the beginning of the 1990s, consolidation activity in the REIT industry has been accelerating. In addition to the existence of only a few studies on this topic, prior research generally suffers from sample sizes being small. Moreover, no study covers any transactions after the year 1998 or outside the US market. The present study overcomes these shortcomings and explicitly includes all international REIT M&A transactions from 1990 until 2005. These broad settings allowed the analysis of a large sample consisting of 107 transactions.

Results of the analysis show that bidders experience small negative abnormal returns, whereas targets exhibit considerable positive abnormal returns, which are highly significant. Although parts of the wealth increase for target shareholders could be the result of a value transfer from bidder to target due to bidders overpaying, in the aggregate, considerable value in the amount of almost $1.6 billion was created for the combined entities. REIT M&A should therefore be viewed positively as they have a beneficial effect for the combined entity.

Furthermore, results indicate that, as expected, there is a considerable difference in returns for the bidders depending on target status. Acquirers of private targets fare much better than those acquiring public targets. These results are concurrent with the blockholder theory and previous findings of Campbell, Ghosh and Sirmans (2001).[340] Returns also exhibit some differences depending

---

340 Cf. Campbell/Ghosh/Sirmans (2001), p. 361–387.

on the country where the transaction took place. Interestingly, there were no cross-border transactions in the REIT industry. Within all transactions both bidder and target were located in the same country. Announcement effects also vary over time with market sentiment. However, this relationship seems to be oppositional for the group of bidders versus the group of targets. This leads to the conclusion that bidders might have overpaid more severely in recent years.

As more and more countries introduce or contemplate introducing their own REIT regimes, empirical research on REIT M&A becomes increasingly important. It will be interesting to observe how the international debate develops and how fast the introduction of new REIT regimes will take place. In any case, REITs will remain an interesting topic for years to come.

V Main Conclusion

V.1 Key Findings and Conclusions

In the past two decades the banking industry has been subject to profound consolidation activity and continues to change rapidly through M&A. Particularly in Europe, the consolidation trend is expected to continue. Numerous M&A transactions could also be witnessed in the related REIT industry, a real estate concept that is becoming more popular and widespread around the world. The large number of M&A transactions in these industries, as well as the considerable transaction volumes involved in both REIT and banking M&A, of course, raises questions on the success of these transactions. Which value implications do these M&A activities have for the shareholders of acquirers? What are the wealth effects for target shareholders? Do these transactions also create value for the combined entity as they should? Finally, what implications do M&A transactions possibly have for rival companies and thereby for the industry as a whole?

A large amount of research has been conducted on the US banking market, but evidence on the consolidation of the European industry is still rather limited. Moreover, evidence on M&A in the related REIT industry is almost non-existent and rather outdated. As a result, there were numerous gaps to fill with empirical evidence in these research areas.

The aim of this doctoral thesis was to identify three interesting research gaps and to fill them with recent empirical evidence. A contribution to existing literature was made in three selected essays on the success of M&A in the banking and REIT industries.

The first essay provided an in-depth analysis of four PSB mergers in Germany. Its positive results on the success of the assessed transactions are only indicative, however, as an analysis of four case studies does not allow general conclusions. This is clearly different for the second and third essays. Here the analyses rely on considerable transaction samples and large numbers of observations. Results can thus be considered noteworthy as they provide interesting insights into the value effects of M&A. In this respect, findings add to existing literature and fill some research gaps on the success of M&A in the banking and REIT industries.

The key findings and conclusions of the three essays as laid out in chapters II, III and IV are summarized in the following:

Essay 1

M&A activity has picked up in recent years and is expected to further increase in the German public banking sector as state guarantees have been repealed (July, 2005). Raised ROE and CIR performance standards have been proclaimed by Germany's PSB association, DSGV, to ensure that PSBs remain competitive. However, the majority of institutes do not anticipate that they can achieve these performance levels on their own. Interestingly, the consolidation trend is confronted with a negative assessment of previous PSB mergers. Both practitioners and researchers generally have a negative view on these transactions. However, prior research in this area is limited. Only two studies, both of which are rather outdated, have previously analyzed mergers in the German public sector.

The first essay adds recent evidence on PSB mergers through an analysis of four exemplary transactions. Results yield a more positive impression of consolidation in the public sector as they illustrate that mergers amongst public savings banks can indeed be successful. The analysis shows that three of the four transactions result in an improvement of ROE in relation to the sector average. Cost synergies could, however, largely not be reaped even three years after the merger, which is understood to be due to limited possibilities for cost cutting measures in these transactions.

Essay 2

The European banking industry has been reshaped by an unprecedented level of consolidation activity since the early 1990s. The majority of transactions/M&A thereby occurred within national borders; cross-border M&A, amongst other things, were perceived as being more difficult and costly. Moreover, regulators and governments attempted to fend off foreign bidders in an attempt to protect domestic banking markets and to foster the creation of national banking champions. The consolidation in Europe's banking industry is, however, expected to increasingly shift towards cross-border M&A, as the sector has historically mainly consolidated domestically and thus remains fragmented on a pan-European level. In addition, cross-border M&A are understood to have become increasingly beneficial as synergies now tend to outweigh incurred costs.

Interestingly, previous research on European cross-border M&A in the banking industry has been rather limited. In addition, no prior study has analyzed rival effects on a European level.

The second essay adds empirical evidence on the success of cross-border M&A and the implications of foreign entry in domestic banking markets. Based on a large number of observations, findings indicate large positive returns for target shareholders and small insignificant returns for bidders' shareholders. On average, the transactions lead to a large positive wealth effect for the combined entity. But most importantly, the analysis indicates significant and positive wealth effects for European rival banks. This positive wealth effect grows with geographic proximity to the target and is largest in the domestic market, where CAARs amount to almost 3%. Interestingly, this positive effect is expected to mainly derive from anticipated future efficiency spill-over effects, thereby leading to an overall performance improvement at competitors that ultimately renders the banking industry more stable. In light of this evidence, national regulators and governments should not deter foreign bidders, but rather be supportive to their entry into the domestic banking industry.

Essay 3

The REIT industry has experienced significant consolidation since the early 1990s and continues to change rapidly through M&A. Despite ongoing consolidation activity and the sheer size of the industry, hardly any empirical research has analyzed the value implications of REIT M&A. The few existing studies additionally suffer from small sample sizes, the omission of recent years and a general lack of international evidence.

The third essay adds evidence to the literature and fills parts of this research gap. In the first analysis of a large international REIT M&A transaction sample, results indicate a considerable value generation for the combined entity. In the aggregate, the analyzed M&A thus seem to create value. Results also indicate that target shareholders, on average, experience a significant positive revaluation of their shares, whereas negative wealth effects for bidding REIT's shareholders are small and insignificant. In addition, the negative effect for bidder and the positive effects for target shareholders become larger in recent years, indicating that bidders overpaid more severely in this period. Market sentiment thus seems to have an influence on returns (and acquisition prices). Findings further indicate that target status has an influence on size and direction of the observed wealth effects for acquiring REITs. Acquisitions of privately held targets lead to positive abnormal returns for the bidder as opposed to negative returns in the acquisition of public REITs. These findings are understood to be concurrent with block-holder theory.

V.2 Outlook

The results of the three essays yield new insights on the success as well as the value implications of M&A. They contribute to existing literature and fill in some research gaps. Of course the analyses also raise a number of further questions that are outlined below.

Concerning mergers in the German public banking sector, it would be interesting to analyze a larger set of recent merger transactions. The assessment of a larger data sample would be able to provide more meaningful results. In the future, it will be interesting to observe whether PSB mergers can yield the desired synergies making the combined institutes more profitable. As restructuring initiatives in this sector generally must be "softer" and accordingly take more time, extending the observation period beyond three years after the merger could allow to capture long-term restructuring effects (e.g. in personnel costs) in this unique banking sector.

It will also be interesting to observe the acceleration of cross-border M&A activity in the European banking industry during the next few years. Particularly the future role of national regulators and governments should be viewed critically with regard to the findings of the second essay. In the future, the expected growing number of cross-border acquisitions will provide an interesting possibility for further analysis in this area. A larger transaction sample could then be used to measure (particularly) the wealth effects for bidder and target shareholders in European transactions. Moreover, a further analysis of other possible value drivers, such as bidder size or concentration ratios, could deepen the understanding of rival effects. Finally, comparing abnormal returns of e.g. domestic and cross-border as well as horizontal and vertical M&A would allow a clearer allocation of the observed rival effects to the three main hypotheses.

Finally, REIT M&A will become an ever more interesting topic in coming years as the number of REIT regimes around the world increases. As more and more real estate portfolios will be brought to market in a REIT structure and as international markets will mature in the future, a growing number of M&A in this sector can be expected. Once the first cross-border M&A start to occur amongst REITs, it will be interesting to observe how the market will value these transactions in comparison to today's prevalent domestic REIT M&A. In any case, it can be expected that the REIT concept will spread further internationally.

To conclude, this doctoral thesis has analyzed the success and the value implications of M&A in the banking and REIT industries. Results show that the sometimes negative assessment of M&A does not necessarily prevail. All three analyses indicate positive wealth effects for the combined entity, on average, after the merger. M&A are found to generally be value creating in the aggregate.

My results are concurrent with prior research, showing that results for the acquiring shareholders are either insignificant or small negative. Results indicate that managers of bidders sometimes pursue goals which are not especially aimed at shareholder value maximization; managers might sometimes be more interested in raising their private status and income rather than in doing the best for the company and its shareholders. In contrast, target shareholders can generally enjoy significant positive wealth effects from an M&A transaction. Interestingly, cross-border M&A in the banking industry are found to not only impact the directly involved parties, but to also have an effect on rivals. Evidence suggests that this effect is positive and significant and even goes across national borders. This positive effect grows with proximity to the target and is largest amongst domestic rivals. Most importantly, this effect is understood to stem from anticipated future efficiency improvements. The spill-over effects from cross-border M&A thus lead to lasting increased performance levels of the industry. Overall results indicate that both targets and rivals benefit from M&A, whereas bidders do not.

References

Akhigbe, A./Madura, J. (1999): The Industry Effects Regarding the Probability of Takeovers, in: The Financial Review, Vol. 34, No. 3, p. 1–18.

Allen, P. R./Sirmans, C. F. (1987): An Analysis of Gains to Acquiring Firm's Shareholders – The Special Case of Reits, in: Journal of Financial Economics, Vol. 18, No. 1, p. 175–184.

Altunbas, Y./Ibanez, D. M. (2004): Mergers and Acquisitions and Bank Performance in Europe – The Role of Strategic Similarities, Working Paper Series No. 398, October 2004, European Central Bank.

Altunbas, Y./Molyneux, P. (1996): Cost Economies in EU Banking Systems, in: Journal of Economics and Business, Vol. 48, No. 3, p. 217–230.

Ambrose, B. W./Ehrlich, S. R./Hughes, W. T./Wachter, S. M. (2000): REIT Economies of Scale: Fact or Fiction, in: Journal of Real Estate Finance and Economics, Vol. 20, No. 2, p. 211–224.

Ambrose, B. W./Linneman, P. (2001): REIT Organizational Structure and Operating Characteristics, in: Journal of Real Estate Research, Vol. 21, No. 3, p. 141–162.

A.T. Kearney (2002): "Wenn's ums Geld geht" – Wege zur Ergebnisverbesserung deutscher Sparkassen, <http://www.atkearney.de/content/misc/wrap per.php/id/48595/name/pdf_wenns_m_geld_geht_1046116298c308.pdf>, accessed on: 10.02.2005.

Atkins, T. (2005): Unicredito deal could challenge cross-border myths, in: Reuters News, 7 June, 2005.

Bales, K. (1993): Rechtliche Aspekte bei der Fusion von Sparkassen, in: Zeitschrift für das gesamte Kreditwesen, Vol. 46, p. 520–524.

Bank for International Settlements (ed.) (2001): Report on Consolidation in the Financial Sector, January 2001, Basel.

Baxmann, U. G. (1995): Kreditwirtschaftliche Betriebsgrößen, Habil., Stuttgart.

Becker, D. (1997): Bewertung von Bankakquisitionen unter Einbeziehung von Zusammenschlusseffekten, Diss., Berlin.

Beitel, P. (2002): Akquisitionen und Zusammenschlüsse europäischer Banken – Wertsteigerung durch M&A-Transaktionen, Diss., Wiesbaden.

Beitel, P./Lorenz, J./Schiereck, D. (2005): Wertsteigerung durch Mergers & Akquisitions, in: Strohmer, M. F. (ed.): International Mergers and Acquisitions, Frankfurt, p. 13–25.

Beitel, P./Schiereck, D. (2003): Zum Erfolg von Akquisitionen und Zusammen-schlüssen zwischen Banken – Eine Bestandsaufnahme der empirischen For-schung, in: Österreichisches Bankarchiv, Vol. 51, p. 501–515.

Beitel, P./Schiereck, D. (2006): Value Creation by Domestic and Cross-border M&A Transactions in the European Banking Market, in: The ICFAI Journal of Mergers & Acquisitions, Vol. 3, No. 3, p. 7–29.

Beitel, P./Schiereck, D./Wahrenburg, M. (2004): Explaining M&A Success in European Banks, in: European Financial Management, Vol. 10, No. 1, p. 109–139.

Belaisch, A./Kodres, L. E./Levy, J./Ubide, A. J. (2001): Euro-Area Banking at the Crossroads, IMF Working Paper No. 28, International Monetary Fund.

Bentele, K. (2003): Bündelung der Kräfte: Ja – aber wie? Zum Grundverständnis des Sparkassenverbundes, in: Vorstand der Kreissparkasse Köln (ed.): Jubi-läumsschrift 150 Jahre Kreissparkasse Köln, Cologne, p. 12–22.

Berger, A. N./Demsetz, R. S./Strahan, P. E. (1999): The consolidation of the fi-nancial services industry: Causes, consequences, and implications for the fu-ture, in: Journal of Banking & Finance, Vol. 23, p. 135–194.

Berger, A. N./DeYoung, R./Udell, G. F. (2001): Efficiency barriers to the con-solidation of the European financial services industry, in: European Financial Management, Vol. 7, No. 1, p. 117–130.

Bikker, J. A./Wesseling, A. A. T. (2003): Intermediation, integration and interna-tionalization: a survey on banking in Europe, Research Series Supervision No. 53, De Nederlandsche Bank.

Bley, J./Madura, J. (2003): Intra-Industry and Inter-Country Effects of European Mergers, in: Journal of Economics and Finance, Vol. 27, No. 3, p. 373–395.

Boehmer, E./Musumeci, J./Poulsen, A. B. (1991): Event-study methodology un-der conditions of event induced variance, in: Journal of Financial Economics, Vol. 30, No. 2, p. 253–272.

Bohl, M. T./Havrylchyk, O./Schiereck, D. (2006): Foreign Acquisitions and Industry Wealth Effects of Privatization: Evidence from the Polish Banking Industry, in: Balling, M./Lierman, F./Mullineux, A. (ed.): Stability and Effi-ciency of Financial Markets in Central and Eastern Europe, Routledge, p. 80–95.

Bosse, B. R. (1982): Rechtsprobleme des Zusammenschlusses von Sparkassen, Berlin.

Bremke, K./Fuß, C./Röckemann, C./Schiereck, D. (2004): Post Merger Integrati-on – Fehlende Exzellenz im deutschen Bankensektor, in: Mergers and Acqui-sitions Review, Issue 8/9, p. 366–369.

Brown, S./Warner, J. (1985): Using daily stock returns: The case of event stud-ies, in: Journal of Financial Economics, Vol. 14, No. 1, p. 3–31

Bundesverband Deutscher Banken (ed.) (2004): Banken 2004 – Fakten, Meinungen, Perspektiven, Berlin.

Büschgen, H. E. (1998): Bankgeschäfte und Bankmanagement, 5th edition, Wiesbaden.

Bundesverband Investment und Asset Management (BVI) (ed.) (2006): Investment 2006 – Daten, Fakten, Entwicklungen, Frankfurt.

Cabral, I./Dierick, F./Vesala, J. (2002): Banking Integration in the Euro Area, Occasional Paper Series No. 6, December 2002, European Central Bank.

Calomiris, C. W. (1999): Gauging the efficiency of bank consolidation during a merger wave, in: Journal of Banking & Finance, Vol. 23, No. 2, p. 615–621.

Calomiris, C. W./Karceski, J. (1998): Is the Bank Merger Wave of the 1990s Efficient? – Lessons from Nine Case Studies, The AEI Press, Washington.

Campa, J. M./Hernando, I. (2004): Shareholder Value Creation in European M&As, in: European Financial Management, Vol. 10, No. 1, p. 47–81.

Campa, J. M./Hernando, I. (2005): The Reaction by Industry Insiders to M&As in the European Financial Industry, Working Paper, Preliminary Draft, December 2005.

Campa, J. M./Hernando, I. (2006): M&As Performance in the European Financial Industry, in: Journal of Banking & Finance, Vol. 30, Issue 12, p. 3367–3392.

Campbell, R. D./Ghosh, C./Sirmans, C. F. (1998): The great REIT consolidation: Fact or Fancy? in: Real Estate Finance, Vol. 15, Issue 2, p. 45–54.

Campbell, R. D./Ghosh, C./Sirmans, C. F. (2001): The Information Content of Method of Payment in Mergers: Evidence from Real Estate Investment Trusts (REITs), in: Real Estate Economics, Vol. 29, No. 3, p. 361–387.

Campbell, R. D./Petrova, M./Sirmans, C. F. (2003): Wealth Effects of Diversification and Financial Deal Structuring: Evidence from REIT Property Portfolio Acquisitions, in: Real Estate Economics, Vol. 31, No. 3, p. 347–366.

Campbell, R. D./Sirmans, C. F. (2002): Policy implications of structural options in the development of real estate investment trusts in Europe, in: Journal of Property Investment & Finance, Vol. 20, No. 4, p. 388–405.

Caruso, A./Palmucci, F (2005): Measuring value creation in bank mergers and acquisitions, Working Paper, University of Bologna.

Chang, S. (1998): Takeovers of Privately Held Targets, Methods of Payment, and Bidder Returns, in: Journal of Finance, Vol. 53, No. 2, p. 773–784.

Claessens, S./Demirgüc-Kunt, A./Huizinga, H. (2001): How does foreign entry effect domestic banking markets? in: Journal of Banking & Finance, Vol. 25, No. 5, p. 891–911.

Cournot, A. A. (1838): Recherches sur les principes mathématiques de la théorie des richesses, Lyon.

Crocker, D. (1998): Inside the Revolution, in: Wharton Real Estate Review, Vol. 2, No. 2, p. 28–33.

Cybo-Ottone, A./Murgia, M. (2000): Mergers and shareholder wealth in European banking, in: Journal of Banking & Finance, Vol. 24, No. 6, p. 831–859.

Dagott, M.-P. (2002): Transsektorale Unternehmensverbindungen zwischen Sparkassen und Genossenschaftsbanken, Diss., Lüneburg.

DeLong, G. L. (2001): Stockholder gains from focusing versus diversifying bank mergers, in: Journal of Financial Economics, Vol. 59, Issue 2, p. 221–252.

Deutsche Bundesbank (ed.) (2004): Die Ertragslage der deutschen Kreditinstitute im Jahr 2003, <www.bundesbank.de/download/volkswirtschaft/mba/2004/200409mba_ertragslage.pdf>, accessed on: 05.01.2005.

Deutsches Institut für Wirtschaftsforschung (DIW) (2004): Untersuchung der Grundlagen und Entwicklungsperspektiven des Bankensektors in Deutschland (Dreisäulensystem), Berlin.

Dodd, P./Warner, J. (1983): On Corporate Governance – A Study of Proxy Contests, in: Journal of Financial Economics, Vol. 11, p. 401–438.

Drost, F. M. (2007): Bund bleibt hart bei Reits, in: Handelsblatt Finanzzeitung, No. 11, 16.01.2007, p. 21, 24.

Deutscher Sparkassen- und Giroverband (2002): Strategie der Sparkassen-Finanzgruppe – Strategische Leitlinien und konkrete Handlungsfelder, Berlin.

Eckbo, B. E. (1983): Horizontal Mergers, Collusion, and Stockholder Wealth, in: Journal of Financial Economics, Vol. 11, Issue 1, p. 241–273.

Eckbo, B. E. (1985): Mergers and the Market Concentration Doctrine: Evidence from the Capital Market, in: Journal of Business, Vol. 58, No. 3, p. 325–349.

Eckbo, B. E. (1992): Mergers and the Value of Antitrust Deterrence, in: The Journal of Finance, Vol. 47, No. 3, p. 1005–1029.

Elayan, F. A./Young, P. J. (1994): The Value of Control: Evidence from Full and Partial Acquisitions in the Real Estate Industry, in: Journal of Real Estate Finance and Economics, Vol. 8, p. 167–182.

Elsas, R. (2004): Preemptive distress resolution through bank mergers, in: Working Paper Series Finance and Accounting 137, Department of Finance, Johann Wolfgang Goethe Universität, Frankfurt.

Ernst & Young (ed.) (2003): Banken in Deutschland – Quo Vadis?, Munich.

European Central Bank (ed.) (2000): Mergers and Acquisitions involving the EU banking industry – facts and implications, Frankfurt.

European Central Bank (ed.) (2004): Report on EU Banking Structure, November 2004, Frankfurt.

Faccio, M./McConnell, J. J./Stolin, D. (2006): Returns to Acquirers of Listed and Unlisted Targets, in: Journal of Financial and Quantitative Analysis, Vol. 41, No. 1, p. 197–220.

Fama, E. (1970): Efficient capital markets: A review of theory and empirical work, in: Journal of Finance, Vol. 25, No. 3, p. 383–417.

Fama, E. (1976): Efficient Capital Markets: Reply, in: Journal of Finance, Vol. 31, No. 1, p. 143–145

Fee, C. E./Thomas, S. (2004): Sources of gains in horizontal mergers: evidence from customer, supplier, and rival firms, in: Journal of Financial Economics, Vol. 74, Issue 3, p. 423–460.

Fischer, M./Lanz, St. (2004): Finanzkennzahlen bei Banken – zwischen Erkenntnis und Illusion, in: Fischer, Matthias (ed.): Handbuch Wertmanagement in Banken und Versicherungen, Wiesbaden, p. 355–390.

Flewelling, S. G./Spiessbach, M. F. (1982): Immobilien über Anteilsscheine, in: Jansen, D. E./Mattern, A. (ed.): Immobilienanlagen in den USA – Investition mit Zukunft, Munich, p. 256–272.

Focarelli, D./Panetta, F./Salleo, C. (2002): Why Do Banks Merge? in: Journal of Money, Credit, and Banking, Vol. 34, No. 4, p. 1047–1066.

Gardener, E. P. M./Molyneux, P./Moore, B. (1998): The Strategic Implications of EMU for European Banking, in: The Service Industries Journal, Vol. 18, No. 4, p. 87–108.

Geiger, H. (1992): Die deutsche Sparkassenorganisation, 2nd edition, Frankfurt.

Gerke, W. (2004): Das Drei-Säulen-System im historischen Zeitraffer, in: Vorstand der Kreissparkasse Köln (ed.): Jubiläumsschrift 150 Jahre Kreissparkasse Köln, Cologne, p. 22–41.

Going Public (2006): Special Edition on REITs, March 2006.

Gold, C. (1997): Gebietsreformbeeinflußte Fusionen bayrischer Sparkassen, Diss., Göttingen.

Graff, R. A. (2001): Economic Analysis Suggests that REIT Investment Characteristics are Not as Advertised, in: Journal of Real Estate Portfolio Management, Vol. 7, No. 2, p. 99–124.

Greer, G. E./Farrell, M. D. (1988): Investment Analysis for Real Estate Decisions, 2nd ed., Chicago.

Haasis, H. (2002): Fusionen zur Gestaltung eines zukunftsfähigen Sparkassensektors – Notwendigkeit und Grenzen, in: Zeitschrift für das Gesamte Kreditwesen, 01.01.2002, p. 29–35.

Hackethal, A. (2003): German banks – a declining industry?, CFS Working Paper No. 2003/27, Johann Wolfgang Goethe Universität, Frankfurt.

Hackethal, A./Schmidt, R. H. (2005): Structural Changes in the German Banking System, Working Paper Series Finance & Accounting 147, Johann Wolfgang Goethe Universität, Frankfurt.

Hadlock, C./Houston, J. F./Ryngaert, M. D. (1999): The role of managerial incentives in bank acquisitions, in: Journal of Banking & Finance, Vol. 23, No. 2–4, p. 221–249.

Haight, G. T./Ford, D. A. (1987): REITs – New Opportunities in Real Estate Investment Trust Securities, Chicago.

Haun, B. (1996): Fusionseffekte bei Sparkassen, Diss., Wiesbaden.

Houston, J. F./Ryngaert, M. D. (1994): The overall gains from large bank mergers, in: Journal of Banking & Finance, Vol. 18, No. 6, p. 1155–1176.

Huang, Y./Walkling, R. A. (1987): Target Abnormal Returns Associated with Acquisition Announcements: Payment, Acquisition Form, and Managerial Resistance, in: Journal of Financial Economics, Vol. 19, p. 329–249.

Hubbard, R. G./Palia, D. (1995): Executive Pay and Performance: Evidence from the US banking industry, in: Journal of Financial Economics, Vol. 39, Issue. 1, p. 105–130.

Huebner, A. (1999): Für Sparkassen in Bayern ist der Wirtschaftsraum neuer Maßstab, in: VWD, 25.11.1999, w/p.

International Monetary Fund (2003): Germany: Article III Consultation – Staff Report; Staff Supplement; and Public Information Notice on the Executive Board Discussion, IMF Country Report No. 03/341, Washington.

Ismail, A./Davidson, I. (2005): Further analysis of mergers and shareholder wealth effects in European banking, in: Applied Financial Economics, Vol. 15, Issue 1, p. 13–30.

Jayratne, J./Strahan, P. E. (1998): Entry Restrictions, Industry Evolution, and Dynamic Efficiency: Evidence from Commercial Banking, in: Journal of Law and Economics, Vol. 41, Issue 1, p. 239–273.

Jensen, M. C. (1986): Agency Costs of Free Cash Flow, Corporate Finance, and Takeovers, in: American Economic Review, Vol. 76, Issue 2, p. 323–329.

Jensen, M. C./Ruback, R. S. (1983): The Market for Corporate Control: The Scientific Evidence, in: Journal of Financial Economics, Vol. 11, p. 5–50.

Khotari, S. P./Warner, J. B. (2004): Econometrics of Event Studies, Working Paper, Tuck School of Business as Dartmouth, p. 1–47.

King, W. B. (1998): REITs as Legal Entities, in: Garrigan, R. T./Parsons, J. F. C. (eds.): Real Estate Investment Trusts, New York, p. 31–82.

Kirchhoff, M./Schiereck, D./Mentz, M. (2006): Market Valuation of Real Estate Finance Mergers – A Note, in: Journal of Property Investment & Finance, forthcoming, w/p.

Kositzki, A. (2004): Das öffentlich-rechtliche Kreditgewerbe – Eine empirische Analyse zur Struktureffizienz und Unternehmensgröße im Sparkassensektor, Dissertation, Wiesbaden.

Kreissparkasse Bamberg (ed.) (2000): Jahresbericht 1999, Bamberg.

Lepetit, L./Patry, S./Rous, P. (2004): Diversification versus specialization: an event study of M&As in the European banking industry, in: Applied Financial Economics, Vol. 14, Issue 9, p. 663–669.

Li, J./Elayan, F. A./Meyer, T. O. (2001): Acquisitions by Real Estate Investment Trusts as a Strategy for Minimization of Investor Tax Liability, in: Journal of Economics and Finance, Vol. 25, No. 1, p. 115–134.

Linneman, P. (1997): Forces Changing the Real Estate Industry Forever, in: Wharton Real Estate Review, Vol. 1, No. 1, p. 1–12.

Maris, B. A./Elayan, F. A. (1990): Capital Structure and the Cost of Capital for Untaxed Firms: The Case of REITs, in: AREUEA Journal, Vol. 18, No. 1, p. 22–39.

McIntosh, W./Officer, D. T./Born, J. A. (1989): The Wealth Effects of Merger Activities: Further Evidence from Real Estate Investment Trusts, in: Journal of Real Estate Research, Vol. 4, No. 3, p. 141–155.

McIntosh, W./Ott, S. H./Liang, Y. (1995): The Wealth Effects of Real Estate Transactions: The Case of REITs, in: Journal of Real Estate Finance and Economics, Vol. 10, p. 299–307.

McWilliams, A./Siegel, D. (1997): Event Studies in Management Research: Theoretical and Empirical Issues, in: Academy of Management Journal, Vol. 40, No. 3, p. 321–337.

NAREIT (2006): Historical REIT Industry Market Capitalization: 1972–2005, <http://www.nareit.com/library/industry/marketcap.cfm>, accessed on: 05.12.2006.

Nash, J. F. (1950): Equilibrium Points in N-person Games, in: Proceedings of the National Academy of Sciences, Vol. 36, p. 48–49.

Paul, S. (2004): Finanzierungsbedarf im Mittelstand – Zwang zur Neupositionierung von Sparkassen?, in: Schäfer, B. (ed.): Handbuch Regionalbanken, Wiesbaden, p. 279–328.

Perez, D./Salas-Fumar, V./Saurina, J. (2005): Banking Integration in Europe, Working Paper No. 0519, Banco de Espana.

Peterson, P. (1989): Event Studies: A Review of Issues and Methodology, in: Quarterly Journal of Business and Economics, Vol. 28, No.3, p. 36–66.

Pilloff, S. J. (1996): Performance Changes and Shareholder Wealth Creation Associated with Mergers of Publicly Traded Banking Institutions, in: Journal of Money, Credit, and Banking, Vol. 28, No. 3, p. 294–310.

Pilloff, S. J./Santomero, A. M. (1998): The value effects of bank mergers and acquisitions, in: Amihud, Y./Miller, G. (eds.): Bank Mergers & Acquisitions, Norwell, p. 59–78.

Polewski, M. (1994): Erfolgreiches politisches Fusionsmanagement als Basis für die gemeinsame Arbeit, in: Benölken, H./Winkelmann, A. (eds.): Fusionsmanagement in der Kreditwirtschaft, Stuttgart, p. 119–129.

Prager, R. A./Hannan, T. H. (1998): Do substantial horizontal mergers generate significant price effects? Evidence from the banking industry, in: The Journal of Industrial Economics, Vol. 46, No. 4, p. 433–452.

Rehkugler, H. (2003): Die Immobilien-AG: Bewertung und Marktattraktivität, Munich.

Rhodes-Kropf, M./Viswanathan, S. (2007): Market Valuation and Merger Waves, in: Journal of Finance, forthcoming, w/p.

Röckemann, C./Schiereck, D. (2004): Im Fusionsprozess agieren deutsche Banken zu zögerlich, in: Börsenzeitung, No. 104, 02.06.2004, p. 4.

Roll, R. (1986): The Hubris Hypothesis of Corporate Takeovers, in: Journal of Business, Vol. 59, Issue 2, p. 197–216.

Sahin, O. F. (2005): The Performance of Acquisitions in the Real Estate Investment Trust Industry, in: Journal of Real Estate Research, Vol. 27, No. 3, p. 321–342.

Sander, H./Kleimeier, S. (2001): Towards a Single Retail Banking Market? New Evidence of Euroland, LIFE Working Paper 01–002, Limburg Institute of Financial Economics.

Sauer, H. D. (2004): Fusionen und notwendige Größe im Wettbewerb aus Sicht einer Landesbank, in: Fischer, M. (ed.): Handbuch Wertmanagement in Banken und Versicherungen, Wiesbaden, p. 165–174.

Schäfer, B. (2004): Wertsteigerung durch Fusion am Beispiel der Sparkasse Hannover, in: Fischer, M. (ed.): Handbuch Wertmanagement in Banken und Versicherungen, Wiesbaden, p. 175–184.

Schierenbeck, H. (1994): Ertragsorientiertes Bankmanagement, 4th edition, Bern.

Schierenbeck, H./Tegeder, P. (2004): Fusionen als Instrument zur Erreichung optimaler Betriebsgrößen in einer europäischen Regionssparkasse, in: Schäfer, Bernhard (ed.): Handbuch Regionalbanken, Wiesbaden, p. 121–148.

Schimmer, Arne (2003): Sparkasse Mainfranken Würzburg: Plädoyer für eine "sanfte Fusion", in: Bank und Markt & Technik, 01.10.2003, p. 23.

Schlierbach, H. (1998): Das Sparkassenrecht in der Bundesrepublik Deutschland, 4th ed., Stuttgart.

Schnatterer, E. (1994): Fusionsszenarien – Fusionstendenzen in den Sektoren, in: Benölken, H./Winkelmann, A. (eds.): Fusionsmanagement in der Kreditwirtschaft, Stuttgart, p. 61–77.

Schranz, M. S. (1993): Takeovers Improve Firm Performance: Evidence from the Banking Industry, in: Journal of Political Economy, Vol. 101, Issue 2, p. 299–326.

Sera, A. (2002): Event Study Tests – A Brief Survey, Working Paper, University of Porto.

Serra, D. (2005): An Investment Guide to European Banks, Morgan Stanley Equity Research, 5–8 April, 2005.

Serra, D./Yucemen, E./Babinet, S./Taliente, D. (2005): European Banking Consolidation: IT Synergies and Basel II Will Drive Cross-Border Restructuring, Morgan Stanley Equity Research and Mercer Oliver Wyman, February 2005,

Serra, D./Zadra, G. (2005): Upgrade UCI to Overweight; We Like the Deal with HVB, Morgan Stanley Equity Research, 13 June, 2005.

Sharur, H. (2003): Industry Structure and Horizontal Takeovers: Analysis of Wealth Effects on Rivals, Suppliers, and Corporate Customers, Working Draft, December 2003, Bentley College.

Shleifer, A./Vishny, R. W. (1986): Large Shareholders and Corporate Control, in: Journal of Political Economy, Vol. 94, No. 3, p. 461–488.

Shleifer, A./Vishny, R. W. (2003): Stock market driven acquisitions, in: Journal of Financial Economics, Vol. 70, No. 3, p. 295–311.

Singal, V. (1996): Airline Mergers and Competition: An Integration of Stock and Product Price Effects, in: Journal of Business, Vol. 69, No. 2, p. 233–269.

Smith, R. C./Walter, I. (1998): Global Patterns of Mergers and Acquisition Activity in the Financial Services Industry, in: Amihud, Y./Miller, G. (eds.): Bank Mergers & Acquisitions, Norwell, p.21–37.

Song, M. H./Walkling, R. A. (2000): Abnormal returns to rivals of acquisition targets: A test of the 'acquisition probability hypothesis', in: Journal of Financial Economics, Vol. 55, p. 143–171.

Sparkasse Bamberg (ed.) (2000): Jahresbericht 1999, Bamberg.

Sparkasse Bamberg (ed.) (2001): Jahresbericht 2000, Bamberg.

Sparkasse Bamberg (ed.) (2002): Jahresbericht 2001, Bamberg.

Sparkasse Coesfeld (ed.) (1997): Jahresbericht 1996, Dülmen.

Sparkasse Mainfranken Würzburg (ed.) (2001): Jahresbericht 2000, Würzburg.

Sparkasse Mainfranken Würzburg (ed.) (2004): Jahresbericht 2003, Würzburg.

Sparkasse Westmünsterland (ed.) (2006): Sparkasse Westmünsterland – Unternehmensportrait, <http://www.sparkassewestmuensterland.de/6306151eb6d30 c9c/index1.htm>, accessed on: 01.10.2006.

Stigler, G. J. (1964): A Theory of Oligopoly, in: The Journal of Political Economy, Vol. 72, No. 1, p. 44–61.

Stillman, R. (1983): Examining Antitrust Policy Towards Horizontal Mergers, in: Journal of Financial Economics, Vol. 11, Issue 1, p. 225–240.

Süchting, J. (1999): Der Sparkassen-Zweckverband aus betriebswirtschaftlicher Sicht, in: Wissenschaftsförderung der Sparkassenorganisation e.V. (ed.): Der

Zweckverband als Organisationsform kommunaler Sparkassen, Stuttgart, p. 89–99.

Tebroke, H.-J. (1993): Größe und Fusionserfolg von Genossenschaftsbanken. Eine theoretische und empirische Analyse der Auswirkungen von Betriebsgröße und fusionsbedingter Betricbsgrößenerweiterung auf die Ergebnisstruktur von Kreditgenossenschaften, Diss., Köln.

The Boston Consulting Group (ed.) (2004): Winners in the age of titans – creating value in banking 2004, Frankfurt/New York/Sydney.

Tourani-Rad, A./van Beek, L. (1999): Market Valuation of European Bank Mergers, Vol. 17, Issue 5, p. 532–540.

Travlos, N. G. (1987): Corporate Takeover Bids, Methods of Payment, and Bidding Firms' Stock Returns, in: Journal of Finance, Vol. 42, No. 4, p. 943–963.

Tröger, N. H. (2003): Mergers & Acquisitions im deutschen Bankensektor, Diss., Wiesbaden.

Trosky, A. (1996): Deutsche Kreditinstitute aus institutionenübergreifender Sicht, Dissertation, Hamburg.

Tross, F./Fröhlich, B. (2006): Konzeption von REITs – Erfahrungen mit der Einführung von REITs international überwiegend positiv, in: Going Public, March 2006, p. 14–15.

UBS (2004): Real Estate Investment Trusts – Time is now, London.

Vander Vennet, R. (1997): Determinants of EU bank takeovers: a logit analysis, Working Paper No. 29, University of Gent.

Väth, A. (1999): Die Grundstücks-Investmentaktiengesellschaft als Pendant zum REIT – Entwicklung einer Konzeption auf Basis der KAAG-Novelle '98, Wiesbaden.

W/A (2000a): Vier unterfränkische Banken fusionieren, in: Süddeutsche Zeitung, 22.1.2000, p. 56.

W/A (2000b): Rhein-Neckar-Nord fast perfekt – Sparkassenfusion Mannheim und Weinheim auf der Zielgraden, in: Börsenzeitung, Nr. 143, 27.07.2000, p. 9.

W/A (2001a): Bildung von Ballungsraumsparkassen wahrscheinlich, in: Handelsblatt, Nr. 164, 27.08.2001, p. 19.

W/A (2001b): Mannheim bleibt interessant, in: Zeitschrift für das gesamte Kreditwesen, 01.02.2001, p. 110.

W/A (2001c): Sparkasse Mannheim nicht über den Berg, in: Financial Times Deutschland, 12.10.2001, p. 24.

W/A (2003a): Losgelöst vom Mannheimer Sanierungsfall; Sparkasse Rhein Neckar steigert Gewinn aus eigener Kraft – Durch Garantien noch bis 2007 geschützt, in: Börsenzeitung, Nr. 181, 19.9.2003, p. 18.

148

W/A (2003b): Der Bankenmarkt wird sich massiv verändern, in: Welt am Sonntag, <http://www.wams.de/data/2003/12/07/207381.html?s=1>, 07.12.2003, accessed on: 01.02.2005.

W/A (2004a): Betriebsbedingte Kündigungen wird es nicht geben, in: Generalanzeiger-Bonn, 24.03.2004, p. 22.

W/A (2004b): Wie geht es der Sparkasse Mannheim heute?, in: Zeitschrift für das Gesamte Kreditwesen, 01.05.2004, p. 470.

W/A (2004c): Köln und Bonn ergänzen sich, in: Handelsblatt, No. 252, 28.12.2004, p. 17.

W/A (2005): Sparkasse Köln-Bonn sieht positive Fusionseffekte, in: Börsenzeitung, No. 14, 21.01.2005, p. 4.

Walter, I. (2004): Mergers and acquisitions in banking and finance: What works, what fails, and why, Oxford.

Weiler, H./Fritsch, W. (2004): Die Chancen von Fusionen zwischen Sparkassen als Handlungsalternative aus Sicht der Sparkasse Nürnberg, in: Fischer, M. (ed.): Handbuch Wertmanagement in Banken und Versicherungen, Wiesbaden, p. 215–226.

Williams, D./Thurm, G. (2004): German banks – a guide to consolidation and structural change, Morgan Stanley Equity Research, March 15, 2004.

Wolfers, B./Kaufmann, M. (2004): Öffentlich-rechtliche Rahmenbedingungen und Umstrukturierungsmodelle für Landesbanken und Sparkassen, in: Fischer, M. (ed.): Handbuch Wertmanagement in Banken und Versicherungen, Wiesbaden, p. 201–214.

Young, P. J./Elayan, F. A. (2002): An Investigation into the Shareholder Wealth Effects of REIT Acquisitions, in: Real Estate Finance, December 2002, p. 27–32.

Zentrum für Europäische Wirtschaftsforschung (ZEW)/ebs (ed.) (2005): Real Estate Investment Trusts: Internationale Erfahrungen und Best Practice für Deutschland, Mannheim.

Zietz, E. N./Sirmans, G. S./Friday, H. S. (2003): The Environment and Performance of Real Estate Investment Trusts, in: Journal of Real Estate Portfolio Management, Vol. 9, No. 2, p. 127–165.